The Outbreak of World War I

CAUSES AND RESPONSIBILITIES

Sixth Edition

*Revised, Edited, and
with an Introduction by*
Holger H. Herwig
The University of Calgary

D0807626

Houghton Mifflin Company   Boston   New York

Editor-in-Chief: Jean L. Woy
Associate Editor: Keith Mahoney
Senior Project Editor: Susan Westendorf
Associate Production Coordinator: Deborah Frydman
Director of Manufacturing: Michael O'Dea
Marketing Manager: Clint Crockett

Cover Design: Alwyn Valásquez, Lapis Design
Cover Art: Nevinson: La Mitrailleuse, 1915, The Bridgman
Art Library, London

Printed in the U.S.A.

Library of Congress Catalog Number: 96-76909

ISBN: 0-669-41692-4

23456789-DH-00 99 98 97

Sure are the causes of war.
Virgil, *Aeneid*

Preface

An intensive debate concerning the origins of World War I has raged throughout the historical profession over the past three decades. Encouraged or outraged by Fritz Fischer's highly provocative suggestions, scholars have combed the major (and minor) archives of Central Europe to track down the fragments of this puzzle. Now that both sides have fired their best shots, the debate has largely settled down, and the fronts have become clearly delineated. In 1991, it seemed opportune to offer students some of the major interpretations of the post-Fischer debate and some introductory remarks as to where the historiography of the origins of the Great War stands today. That volume represented a significant updating of the interpretations offered by the late Dwight E. Lee in the four editions of *The Outbreak of the First World War* published by D. C. Heath between 1958 and 1975. This sixth edition represents cuts from and additions to the fifth edition suggested by students and reviewers alike.

As far as possible, I have tried to reproduce faithfully the writings of the authors whom I feel best represent a broad spectrum of interpretations. Deletions have been made not to distort meaning but rather to exercise peripheral commentary. English usage was amended to render it more familiar to North American students — again, without changing meaning. Titles, common names, places, and institutions appear in the form given by the original authors. The Chronology of Events presents the most important dates. The list of Principal Proper Names (gleaned both from major historical accounts of the First World War and from well-known biographical dictionaries) as far as possible reproduces the most customary forms.

Finally, I would like to thank my editors at D. C. Heath, James Miller and Lauren Johnson, for their steadfast counsel and good cheer. My wife, Lorraine, once more provided sage advice and severe criticism at all stages of the book.

H. H. H.

Contents

I The Coming of War   14

Chronology of
Events

Principal Proper Names

Apis: *See* Dimitrijević-Apis.

Asquith, Herbert Henry: British Prime Minister, 1908–1915.

Ballplatz [Ballhausplatz]: Site in Vienna of the Ministry of Foreign Affairs and hence a synonym for it.

Berchtold von und zu Ungarschitz, Fratting und Pulitz, Leopold, Count: Austro-Hungarian Minister of Foreign Affairs, 1912–1915.

Bethmann Hollweg, Theobald von: German Chancellor, 1909–1917.

Buchanan, Sir George William: British Ambassador in St. Petersburg, 1910–1917.

Bunsen, Sir Maurice de: British Ambassador in Vienna, 1913–1914.

Carol I: King of Rumania, 1881–1914.

Conrad von Hötzendorf, Field Marshall Franz, Baron (later, Count): Austro-Hungarian Chief of the General Staff, 1906–1911, 1912–1917.

Danilov, General Yury Nikiforovich: Quartermaster-General of the Russian army, 1914–1915.

Delbrück, Clemens von: Prussian Minister of the Interior, 1909–1918.

Dimitrijević-Apis, Colonel Dragutin: Chief of Serbian Military Intelligence, 1913–1916.

Falkenhayn, General Erich von: Prussian Minister of War, 1913–1914; Chief of the German General Staff, 1914–1916.

Foch, General Ferdinand: Commander of the French XX Corps and Chief Assistant to General Joffre, 1914.

Franz [Francis] Ferdinand d'Este, Archduke: Austro-Hungarian heir apparent, 1896–1914.

Franz [Francis] Joseph: Emperor of Austria, 1848–1916; King of Hungary, 1867–1916.

Ganz, Hugo: Austrian journalist.

Giesl von Gieslingen, Wladimir, Baron: Austro-Hungarian Ambassador in Belgrade, 1913–1914.

Goremykin, Ivan Logginovich: Russian Chairman of the Council of Ministers, 1914–1916.

Goschen, Sir William Edward: British Ambassador in Berlin, 1908–1914.

Grey, Sir Edward (later, Viscount Grey of Fallodon): British Secretary for Foreign Affairs, 1905–1916.

Grigorovich, Admiral Ivan Konstantinovich: Russian Minister of the Navy, 1911–1917.

Haldane, Richard Burdon (later, Viscount Haldane of Cloan): British Secretary of State for War, 1905–1912.

Hammann, Otto: Head of the Press Section, German Foreign Office, 1893–1916.

Havenstein, Rudolf: President of the German Reichsbank, 1908–1924.

Heydebrand und der Lasa, Ernst von: German politician.

Hoyos, Alexander, Count: Chief of Cabinet, Austro-Hungarian Foreign Office, 1912–1917.

Jagow, Gottlieb von: German Secretary for Foreign Affairs, 1913–1916.

Janushkevich: *See* Yanushkevich.

Joffre, General Joseph: Chief of the French General Staff, 1911–1916.

Kitchener, Field Marshal Horatio Herbert, Lord: British Secretary of State for War, 1914–1915.

Krivoshein, Aleksandr Vasilevich: Russian Minister of Agriculture, 1908–1915.

Krupp von Bohlen und Halbach, Gustav: German industrialist.

Lerchenfeld-Koefering, Hugo, Count von: Bavarian Representative in Berlin, 1880–1919.

Leuckart von Weissdorf, Traugott, Baron: Saxon Military Plenipotentiary in Berlin, 1911–1917.

Lichnowsky, Karl Max, Prince von: German Ambassador in London, 1912–1914.

Moltke, Field Marshal Helmuth [the Elder], Count von: Chief of the Prussian General Staff, 1857–1888.

Moltke, General Helmuth J. L. [the Younger] von: Chief of the Prussian-German General Staff, 1906–1914.

Müller, Admiral Georg Alexander von: Chief of the German Navy Cabinet, 1906–1918.

Naumann, Viktor: German journalist.

Nicholas II: Tsar of Russia, 1894–1918.

Paléologue, Maurice: French Ambassador in St. Petersburg, 1914–1917.

Pashitch [Pašic], Nikola: Serbian Prime Minister, 1912–1919.

Poincaré, Raymond: French Premier, 1912–1913; President, 1913–1920.

Potiorek, Field Marshal Oskar: Austro-Hungarian Governor in Bosnia-Herzegovina, 1911–1914.

Pourtalès, Friedrich, Count von: German Ambassador in St. Petersburg, 1907–1914.

Quai d'Orsay: Site in Paris of the Ministry of Foreign Affairs and hence a synonym for it.

Rathenau, Walther: German industrialist.

Riezler, Kurt: Counsellor, German Foreign Office, 1906–1920.

Salza und Lichtenau, Ernst, Baron von: Saxon Minister in Berlin, 1911–1914.

Sazonoff [Sazonov], Sergei Dmitrievich: Russian Minister of Foreign Affairs, 1910–1916.

Schlieffen, Field Marshal Alfred, Count von: Chief of the Prussian General Staff, 1891–1905.

Stumm, Wilhelm von: Political Director, German Foreign Office, 1911–1916.

Stürgkh, Karl, Count von: Austrian Prime Minister, 1911–1916.

Südekum, Albert: German politician.

Sukhomlinov, General Vladimir Aleksandrovich: Russian Minister of War, 1909–1915.

Szögyény-Marich, László, Count von: Austro-Hungarian Ambassador in Berlin, 1892–1914.

Tirpitz, Grand Admiral Alfred von: German Secretary of the Navy Office, 1897–1916.

Tisza de Boros-Jenö, István [Stephan], Count: Hungarian Prime Minister, 1913–1917.

Tschirschky und Bögendorff, Heinrich von: German Ambassador in Vienna, 1907–1916.

Viviani, René: French Premier and Minister for Foreign Affairs, June–August 1914.

Waldersee, General Georg, Count von: Quartermaster-General of the Prussian Army, 1912–1914.

Wilhelm II [William II]: German Emperor and King of Prussia, 1888–1918.

Wilhelmstrasse: Site in Berlin of the German Foreign Office and hence a synonym for it.

Yanushkevich, General Nikolai Nikolaevich: Chief of the Russian General Staff, 1914–1915.

Zimmermann, Arthur: German Undersecretary for Foreign Affairs, 1911–1916.

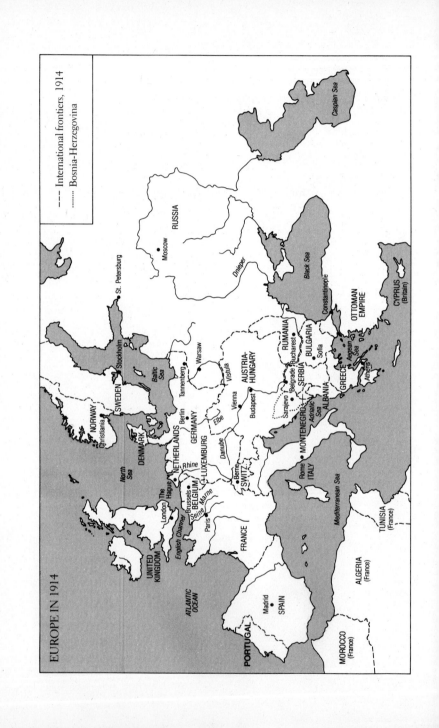

EUROPE IN 1914

--- International frontiers, 1914
.... Bosnia-Herzegovina

RUSSIA

Moscow

St. Petersburg

Dnieper

Black Sea

Constantinople

OTTOMAN
EMPIRE

CYPRUS
(Britain)

Stockholm

Baltic
Sea

Warsaw

Vistula

AUSTRIA-
HUNGARY

RUMANIA

Bucharest

BULGARIA

Sofia

Belgrade

SERBIA

Sarajevo

GREECE

Aegean
Sea

Athens

NORWAY

Christiania

SWEDEN

DENMARK

Berlin

Tannenberg

Elbe

Vienna

Budapest

MONTENEGRO

Adriatic
Sea

ALBANIA

North
Sea

NETHERLANDS

The
Hague

GERMANY

Rhine

Danube

Rome

ITALY

Mediterranean Sea

London

Brussels

BELGIUM

LUXEMBURG

Berne

SWITZ.

TUNISIA
(France)

UNITED
KINGDOM

English Channel

Seine

Marne

Paris

FRANCE

ATLANTIC
OCEAN

ALGERIA
(France)

PORTUGAL

Madrid

SPAIN

MOROCCO
(France)

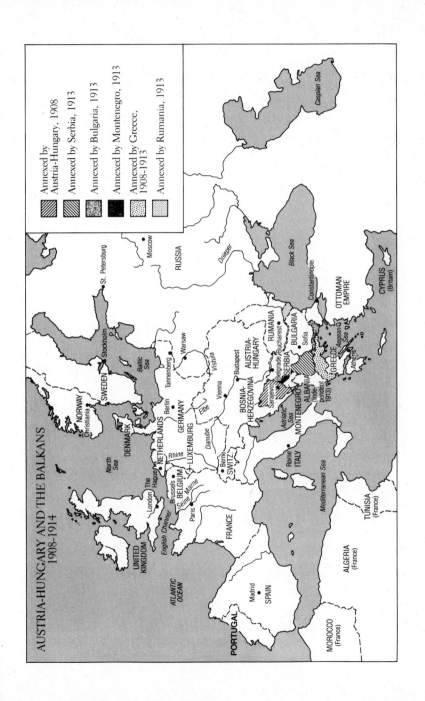

AUSTRIA-HUNGARY AND THE BALKANS
1908-1914

Annexed by
Austria-Hungary, 1908

Annexed by Serbia, 1913

Annexed by Bulgaria, 1913

Annexed by Montenegro, 1913

Annexed by Greece,
1908-1913

Annexed by Rumania, 1913

Introduction

The war solved no problems. Its effects, both immediate and indirect, were either negative or disastrous. Morally subversive, economically destructive, socially degrading, confused in its causes, devious in its course, futile in its result, it is the outstanding example in European history of meaningless conflict.

These eloquent words, applied by the British scholar C. V. Wedgwood to the Thirty Years' War, could equally pertain to the First World War. *La Grande Guerre* was a disaster from which Europe never fully recovered: it fell from being the world's banker to being its greatest debtor; it lost the moral edge both at home and in its colonies; over thirty-seven million casualties prompted contemporaries to speak of a "lost generation." Indeed, the "war to end all wars" was by 1919 given a numerical prefix in order not to confuse it with what might come.

Even victory proved an illusion. The Great War, as most other wars, settled little and brought with it a plethora of new problems. Relatively stable monarchies gave way to a host of petty, ambitious, and squabbling nation states. Habsburg, Hohenzollern, and Romanov yielded to Horthy, Hitler, and Lenin. Was the world better off for it? Nationalism was more virulent than ever. Ethnic hatred flourished. Social Darwinism again raised its ugly head.

What had the major combatants achieved with their sacrifices? Austria-Hungary was no longer a power — much less a great power — and its ramshackle empire was subdivided into about a dozen insecure nation states. France was bled white and left paranoid about security. Great Britain, less secure against American and Japanese competition, faced demands for independence throughout its vast empire. Germany was bankrupt, virtually disarmed, and on the brink of starvation. Italy, barely a victor, felt cheated of the spoils of war. Japan was denied both Germany's Far Eastern colonies and recognition of racial equality by the West. Russia was in the throes of civil war, from which it would recover only to plunge into the nightmare of Stalinist rule. Many of these nations refused to accept the decisions of the Peace of Paris and thereafter regarded war as the only escape from their perceived predicaments.

Apart from being a major turning point in history, Europe's "Great Folly" also had a profound influence upon subsequent events. By placing the blame for the war on Germany and its allies, and by stipulating that they were to pay for the damages incurred by all combatants, the victorious Allied and Associated Powers crippled the Weimar Republic from birth and provided Adolf Hitler and his fellows with a grand propaganda weapon in their campaign to "revise" the Treaty of Versailles.

Not surprisingly, there arose in Germany a fierce battle to refute the so-called "war-guilt lie." Newspapers, magazines, radio broadcasts, and diplomatic missions abroad were utilized to spread the official German version of the origins of the Great War, and thereby to confuse historical understanding. Scholars at home and abroad were engaged to "sanitize" the causes of the war. Documents were destroyed, forged, or "cleansed" to hide the truth. An entire department within the Wilhelmstrasse labored tirelessly to oversee this vast effort at "patriotic self-censorship." The German government, for decades unwilling to face honestly the issue of war guilt, in 1927 tried to deny the legal scholar Hermann Kantorowicz not only publication of his radical findings concerning Germany's role in the origins of the war but also a university chair, and in 1964 successfully held back funds already granted to the historian Fritz Fischer for a scheduled lecture tour in the United States. The German nation — and, by extension, Europe — paid a terrible price for this perversion of knowledge.

Hence, whether inevitably or remarkably, a host of historians, headed by Fritz Fischer, Adolf Gasser, Imanuel Geiss, and John Röhl, among others, in the 1960s reopened the entire historical conundrum not with polemics but with serious archival research in Austria as well as in East and West Germany. Whatever one may think of their findings and conclusions, Fischer and his supporters seized the initiative and defined the parameters of the debate. Neither the visceral reaction of conservative colleagues nor official government censure deterred them.

The "Fischer controversy" is important because it forced the West German establishment, at both academic and governmental levels, to reopen a question that it did not want to face: Germany's accountability for the First World War. While most West German scholars and politicians were willing to accept Hitler's — if not Germany's — responsibility for starting the Second World War, they proved remarkably unwilling to confront the possibility that the same could be said of the First World War. The damage to the Bonn regime's self-image would be devastating: hence, the rebarbative attempts by prominent West German historians such as Gerhard Ritter and Karl Dietrich Erdmann as well as Foreign Minister Gerhard Schröder to prevent the spread of Fritz Fischer's views beyond the Federal Republic.

Continued study of the origins of the Great War is still relevant today. For nearly fifty years after 1945, Europe, as in 1914, was divided roughly equally into two major alliance blocs: the North Atlantic Treaty Organization (NATO) and the Warsaw Pact. Many statesmen and scholars wondered whether the same nefarious impersonal forces that pressed Europe, in the words of David Lloyd George, to "slither" over the brink into the "boiling cauldron of war" might not emerge once more and cause an even greater calamity. Since the *Wende*, or turning point of 1989–1990, the virulent forces of nationalism, racialism, and militarism that proved so prevalent in 1914 seem to have reemerged with a vengeance in Russia and its former border states, and most destructively in Bosnia-Herzegovina. The "causes and responsibilities" for the outbreak of wars are very much with us today, as they were in 1914.

In the 1960s, political scientists, bedazzled by the prospect of simulating political scenarios with computer "games," and ignorant of Fischer's findings, set out eagerly to study the possible causes of a third world war by analyzing the July crisis of 1914. In each case, the end result of the calculations was the same: Europe innocently "slithered" over the brink into war. Yet if one accepts even the most moderate conclusions of the Fischer school, namely, that Germany *opted* for a general European war on and after 5 July 1914, the computer input would be sufficiently altered to lead to a much different result. Nations do not "slither" into wars: human beings at the highest levels of the decision-making process carefully evaluate their chances and decide for war with the full expectation of winning and thereby solving the difficulties that prompted them to consider drawing the sword in the first place. In short, the "1914 analogy" must be rethought and reworked in the light of the actual mindset of German political, diplomatic, and military leaders in 1914.

＊   ＊   ＊

The selections in this book fall into three broad categories: The Coming of War, The Outbreak of War, and The Question of War Guilt. They were selected to present the viewpoints of eminent international scholars, and for the most part constitute succinct summaries of their larger studies. Obviously, not all interpretations could be included; this is especially the case with regard to the East German Marxist scholars associated with Fritz Klein at the *Zentralinstitut für Geschichte* of the *Akademie der Wissenschaften*. Their three-volume indictment, *Germany in the First World War*, published in 1968, is disappointingly predictable: the war was caused by the forces of "monopolistic capitalism," that is, by bankers and industrialists, aided and abetted by their "allies" among the noble East Elbian landowners and the military. Moreover, with the notable exception of documents pertaining to the trade policies of the Imperial Foreign Office, the holdings in the archives of East Germany do not bear directly upon the July crisis of 1914; much of the work of Klein and his associates thus rests on the documentary resources published by Fischer and his allies. Above all, the simplistic monocausal determinism of the East German Marxist school should not obscure from students the complexity of the historical forces that combined to produce the debacle of 1914.

Every effort has been made to present varying points of view in this collection; this is especially true in the case of the "Fischer controversy." If the selections seem heavily Germanocentric, this is because of the parameters of the current debate concerning the origins of the war. No serious scholar today would suggest that Britain, France, Italy, Japan, or Russia was responsible for the war.

In the first reading, James Joll seeks the deeper causes behind the "mood of 1914": long-term patterns of education, the rhetoric of the inevitability of war, invasion scares, and downright fear of the unknown. All of these factors combined to undermine the liberal values of peace and rational resolution of problems.

Michael Howard then analyzes the European state system on

the eve of the Great War. After briefly introducing the diplomats who controlled the levers of power in Vienna, Berlin, St. Petersburg, Paris, and London, Howard turns to their military advisers, who, he suggests, all nurtured one common assumption: that they had a "better-than-evens chance" of winning the war. And they all shared a set of presuppositions: that war was inevitable, that it would be short, and that the best chance for victory lay in the offensive. Finally, Howard shrewdly critiques the vital interests of each of the major powers.

L. L. Farrar, Jr., next argues that the "men of 1914" proved readily willing to accept war partly because of their firm belief that the war would be nothing more than a "short cleansing thunderstorm" (Winston S. Churchill) and because the very nature of the alliance system prompted most continental powers, especially Paris and Vienna, to risk protracted war in the face of possible political collapse.

Arno J. Mayer openly encourages historians to abandon the reams of diplomatic files as well as amateur psychology, and instead to see the origins of the war in the dialectic between domestic tensions and disturbances (prerevolutionary conditions) and the conservative decision-making processes of governments. Along similar lines, Wolfgang J. Mommsen suggests a functional approach: given that the German government structure was devoid of firm direction as a result of crippling domestic influences from both left and right, and because of rapid socioeconomic change, Bethmann Hollweg withdrew into a world of secrecy and opted for war not out of a lust of conquest but out of a sense of domestic weakness and confusion. Mommsen argues that the Hohenzollern monarchy experienced a decided deterioration of its position in the last two years of peace — Social Democratic victory in the elections of 1912, difficulties in getting approval of the largest peacetime army bill ever in 1913, and the civil-military confrontation during the notorious Zabern affair in Alsace-Lorraine — and that as a result, it nurtured thoughts of preventive war against France and Russia.

The second section of selections begins with Joachim Remak's reminder that Serbia provided the catalyst to war. Belgrade, like Vienna, was willing to engage in brinkmanship in July 1914 in the firm belief that the prize — a Great South Slav State — justified the stakes and that with Russia's backing, Serbia just might seize this advantage. Next, Samuel R. Williamson, Jr., admonishes us to keep in mind that the decision for war was made not in Berlin but in Vienna. The latter, he suggests, was more than a marionette, and Berlin less than the driving force behind the war. Berlin did not need to take Vienna "on the leash," as Fischer would have it; rather, Foreign Minister Leopold von Berchtold as well as Chief of the General Staff Franz Conrad von Hötzendorf were willing in the aftermath of Sarajevo to undertake "a calculated risk to open war."

In the lengthiest selection in this book, from Fischer's second book, *War of Illusions*, the Hamburg historian vociferously reiterates his case that Germany opted for war in July, "now or never." Far from willing merely to undertake a "calculated risk," Bethmann Hollweg chose war in order to realize his ambitious scheme of economic and territorial aggrandizement (as later evidenced in the vast annexationist schemes of the infamous September Program). In short, inspired by economic interest, German decision makers, under considerable pressure from right-wing lobbies, deliberately escalated the management of the July crisis into a major war — purposefully choosing not to deescalate it and to produce a diplomatic result short of war.

Wayne C. Thompson, in his study of Bethmann Hollweg's confidant Kurt Riezler, offers selections from Riezler's diary to uphold the thesis of the "calculated risk," that the chancellor was willing to risk the *threat* of a Balkan (or even a European) war in order to diplomatically destroy the Triple Entente. Only when this limited-war strategy proved illusory because Russia refused to stay out of the Austro-Serbian conflict, the argument runs, did the military in Berlin and Vienna press for a major war. It should not be overlooked that since 1983 the originality of the Riezler diary, especially for the critical days of July 1914, has been seriously questioned — a turn of events that added grist to the mills of Fischer and his supporters, who quickly suggested that potentially damaging passages detailing Bethmann Hollweg's "war policy" were expunged by "patriotic self-censors."

The cutting edge of the World War I debate in Germany today lies with countless reexaminations of the "war euphoria" of 1914. Wolfgang Kruse argues that this "euphoria" mainly suffused middle-class professionals and students, and he cautions against accepting at face value contemporary estimates of one million volunteers for the war. Instead, Kruse suggests, countless pastors and police spies reported "depression, frustration, and fear," especially in working-class quarters. Finally, Kruse warns students of the Great War not to fall into the trap of analyzing war enthusiasm along gender lines; men and women alike succumbed to the "spirit of 1914."

The most recent investigation into Russia's role during the July crisis by D. C. B. Lieven concludes that Russian policymakers had no foreknowledge of the conspiracy hatched by Serbian military intelligence to murder Archduke Francis Ferdinand, and that St. Petersburg entered the fray only in the aftermath of Austria-Hungary's severe ultimatum to Belgrade. Fearing for the independence of the Serbian state as well as for Russia's "historic mission" and "prestige in the Balkans," Foreign Minister Sergei Sazonov, with the support of his military and French Ambassador Maurice Paléologue, convinced a wavering Nicholas II to risk a general European war rather than to back down in the face of Austro-German initiatives in the Balkans. Zara Steiner concludes the section with a prescient analysis of how the British Cabinet managed to muddle through to war, owing less to its own resolution than to German insensitivity over respect for Belgian neutrality.

The third section of readings opens with the classic charge of German and Austrian war guilt as laid down in 1919 in Article 231 of the Treaty of Versailles. John Röhl and Imanuel Geiss offer powerful endorsements of Fischer's position. While Röhl reaches all the way back to the alleged "war council" of 8 December 1912 as the point at which German decision makers proved willing to plunge over the brink into war, Geiss sees the July crisis as the crucial point. For both scholars, there can be no doubt whatsoever concerning German responsibility for the war.

As counterpoint, the late Gerhard Ritter suggests not only that Fischer's interpretation of the pertinent documents is inaccurate, but also that Fischer failed to approach his materials with suffficient understanding of their meanings within their historical context. In the end, he considered dissemination of Fischer's views to constitute nothing short of a "national tragedy." Then, in a highly revisionist piece, Paul Schroeder argues that Britain sought to "encircle" not

Germany but Austria-Hungary, and that the Entente powers in 1914 were quite willing to destroy the weakest link in the European concert, the Danubian monarchy. Schroeder again suggests a less Germanocentric view.

The last selection by Holger H. Herwig indicates the dangers of "patriotic self-censorship" and "preemptive historiography" in the German case. Selective editing of documents, destruction of pertinent and possibly damaging records, vendettas against radical scholars, distortion of the truth on the part of both official and semiofficial "censors" served neither historical truth nor the national interest in the long run. Instead, they paved the path for an even greater calamity: Adolf Hitler and the Second World War. Yet the efforts of the "patriotic self-censors" were so successful that as late as 1930, Hermann Hesse informed Thomas Mann of his firm belief that "of 1,000 Germans, even today 999 still know nothing of [our] war guilt." The serious student of history is left to ponder whether a perverse law operates whereby those events that are most important are also hardest to understand because they attract the greatest attention from mythmakers and "patriots."

*   *   *

The First World War did not solve any problems, and its effects were indeed "either negative or disastrous," but unlike the Thirty Years' War, it was not "confused in its causes." It should be clear thirty years after the appearance of Fritz Fischer's *Griff nach der Weltmacht* that Europe did not simply "slither" over the brink of war in July 1914. The "men of 1914" knew well from previous crises the probable scenario of any direct involvement in Balkan affairs on the part of the great powers. The pivotal decision makers of July 1914 may have been mediocre — not the quality of Bismarck, Cavour, Disraeli, or Gladstone — but they were not idiots. Prince Philipp zu Eulenburg-Hertefeld, once the Kaiser's trusted adviser and a man with intimate connections in the highest strata of the decision-making process in Berlin, in September 1919 confidentially imparted to a friend his innermost knowledge of the July crisis:

> *Serbia is Russia. If Austria marches against Serbia and if Berlin does not prevent Austria's belligerent action, then the great breaking wave of World War rolls irresistibly towards us. I repeat: Berlin must know*

that, otherwise idiots *live in the Wilhelmstrasse. Kaiser Wilhelm* must *know that.*

Where, then, does the Fischer controversy stand today? The noted Bielefeld historian Hans-Ulrich Wehler estimated that even his conservative colleagues in the Federal Republic accept about three-fourths of Fischer's assertions. I agree fully with that assessment. On the other hand, Fischer's claims that Germany threw the switches for war during the so-called war council of 8 December 1912, and that 1914 constituted a planned German "grab for world power" remain unacceptable. In fact, there was no systematic planning for war between December 1912 and July 1914 — economically, politically, diplomatically, or psychologically. The chaotic decision-making process in Berlin allowed no such rational long-term preparations; only Wilhelm II had the power required to coordinate such a grand strategy, and, as is well known, he was patently unable to fulfill such a Bismarckian role.

However, Kurt Riezler's celebrated notion of the "calculated risk" is also inadequate to explain the events of July 1914. Quite apart from the likelihood that key passages of his diary for July 1914 were "cleansed" by "patriotic self-censors" in order to obscure German responsibility for starting the war, the central argument that Bethmann Hollweg sought only to bluff the Entente into diplomatic self-destruction is disingenuous. Such a policy had been tried during the first Moroccan crisis and had ended with Germany's resounding diplomatic defeat at Algeciras in 1905; it is hardly conceivable that Berlin could see merit in a repeat performance nine years later. Moreover, it is clear from available sources that the military especially was determined to avoid another major diplomatic humiliation. Professor Annelise Thimme, whose father edited the forty-volume edition of German documents from 1870 to 1914, is on the mark when she depicts the resuscitation of Riezler's mental gymnastics by Andreas Hillgruber in West Germany and Konrad Jarausch in the United States as nothing more than putting "new wine into old wine skins."

In the final analysis, one can attribute responsibility — to be sure, not *sole* responsibility — for the war with some measure of certainty. The regicide at Sarajevo was inspired and supported by Serbian military intelligence, and thus Belgrade must shoulder a good measure of responsibility. Second, Austria-Hungary made the conscious decision to launch a Balkan war in order to reduce Serbia to the status of at best a "semi-protectorate," and to appeal to its ally in Berlin for support in case the Austro-Serbian conflict escalated into a general European war. Unfortunately, Austria-Hungary's culpability for the start of the First World War has been overshadowed for far too long by the intensity of the Fischer controversy, but Samuel Williamson's book on Vienna during the July crisis has redressed the existing imbalance.

The greatest measure of responsibility, however, remains with Germany. Planners, both civilian and military, were all too eager to resolve their perceived diplomatic encirclement by use of force — "now or never," as Wilhelm II put it. Force alone, the argument ran, could secure and expand the Reich's position of semi-hegemony on the Continent as well as offer relief from the paranoidal fear of Russian expansion. For, had there been a genuine desire in Berlin for a diplomatic resolution of the crisis, they had only to accept London's repeated offers to convene a European conference. Instead, Berlin was beset by a "strike-now- better-than-later" mentality that was perhaps best captured by Foreign Secretary Gottlieb von Jagow when he recorded a conversation he had with General von Moltke at the end of May 1914:

> The prospects for the future weighed heavily upon him [Moltke]. In two to three years Russia would have finished arming. Our enemies' military power would then be so great that he did not know how he could deal with it. Now we were still more or less a match for it. In his view there was no alternative but to fight a preventive war so as to beat the enemy while we could still emerge fairly well from the struggle. The Chief of Staff therefore put it to me that our policy should be geared to bringing about an early war.

The simple truth is that top-level decision makers first in Vienna and then in Berlin opted for war after weighing carefully both their chances and their alternatives. Thereafter, planners in St. Petersburg were convinced that Russia's "historic mission" as well as prestige dictated that they take up the challenge posed by Austria-Hungary and Germany — even at the risk of a general European war. France saw no alternative but to support its continental ally. Britain was determined to head off possible German hegemony on the Continent. Italy entered the war for the simplest of all reasons: spoils.

The French philosopher Henri Bergson is credited with the *bon mot* that war in 1914 was impossible but probable. The selections that follow are designed to shed light on the complex matrix of considerations that prompted the "men of 1914" to undertake Europe's "Great Folly."

Variety of Opinion: The Pre-Fischer School

Europe slithered into war:

> *How was it that the world was so unexpectedly plunged into this terrible conflict? Who was responsible? . . . The nations slithered over the brink into the boiling cauldron of war without a trace of apprehension or dismay.*
>
> David Lloyd George

No one was responsible:

> *None of the Powers wanted a European War. . . . But the verdict of the Versailles Treaty that Germany and her allies were responsible for the War, in view of the evidence now available, is historically unsound. It should therefore be revised.*
>
> Sidney Bradshaw Fay

France and Russia are to blame:

> *The chief objects of Russian and French foreign policy, seizure of the [Dardanelles and Bosporus] Straits and the return of Alsace-Lorraine, could be realized only through a general European war. . . . In estimating the order of guilt of the various countries we may safely say that the only direct and immediate responsibility for the World War falls upon Serbia, France and Russia, with the guilt about equally divided.*
>
> Harry Elmer Barnes

Fate willed the war:

> *In every country there was an instinctive feeling that the future, for an indefinite period, was at stake, that the nation which did not play its part would be outdistanced in the eternal competition of peoples, and that any sacrifice must be borne to insure the continuance of historic traditions. In the face of this intense nationalism, which had been born of the French Revolution and intensified by the events of the nineteenth century, pacific instincts, socialistic programmes, religious scruples and humanitarian ideals were of no avail.*
>
> Bernadotte E. Schmitt

Germany and its allies are to blame:

> *The Allied and Associated Governments affirm and Germany accepts the responsibility of Germany and her allies for causing all the loss and damage to which the Allied and Associated Governments and their nationals have been subjected as a consequence of the war imposed upon them by the aggression of Germany and her allies.*

Article 231 of the Treaty of Versailles

"Down With the Monster," French troops attack the German dragon in September 1914. (The Granger Collection)

PART

I

The Coming of War

James Joll

The Mood of 1914

James Joll, holder of the Stevenson Chair of International History at the London School of Economics until his retirement in 1981, has written widely on European intellectual and social history. As well as being British editor in chief of *Documents on German Foreign Policy*, he has published a biography, *Antonio Gramsci*, and analyses of *The Anarchists* and *The Second International*. In this piece, Joll seeks the deeper causes behind the euphoria that accompanied the declaration of war in 1914. It is his argument that long-term patterns of education, the rhetoric of the inevitability of war, invasion scares, and downright fear all contributed to the "mood of 1914," a mood that was in part a revolt against the liberal values of peace and rational problem solving.

From *The Origins of the First World War* by James Joll, 1984, pp. 171–196. Reprinted by permission of Longman Group UK Limited.

Any government, even the most dictatorial, needs to be sure of popular support before starting a war. For this reason, . . . each of the governments which declared war in 1914 was concerned to present its decision in such a way as to win the maximum public approval: the French were fighting to defend the soil of France against a new German invasion; the Germans were fighting to defend the soil of Germany against the Cossack hordes, and so on. But the mood in which the peoples of Europe accepted and in some cases even welcomed the idea of war and temporarily forgot their social and political differences was not just the result of the way in which their governments had justified their immediate political decisions. It was founded on an accumulation of national traditions and attitudes which had formed beliefs about the nature of the state and its authority, reinforced by the curriculum in the schools over the past decades and the kind of language in which politicians and journalists had discussed international relations. The analysis of this complex of beliefs and attitudes and of the accumulated mentality of a nation is a very difficult task.

Still, the evidence which we do have and the studies of attitudes, both popular and governmental, suggest that there are certain factors in all the belligerent countries which contributed to the mood which made war possible. Although there had been . . . a series of international crises, which, at least since 1905, had caused talk of war, and although some writers and most generals and admirals believed in the inevitability of international conflict, the crisis of July 1914 when it came was a shock to many people who were given little time to reflect on what was actually happening. Indeed, observers of the state of international relations had found the situation in the early months of 1914 more encouraging than for several years: the effects of the Balkan wars had been more or less contained without conflict between the Great Powers; the Zabern affair, which might have been expected to increase tension between France and Germany, had been received comparatively calmly in France: although the naval rivalry between England and Germany still provoked rhetorical phrases on both sides, there were some signs that the pace of naval building might be about to slacken, and the two countries were negotiating amicably about the Portuguese colonies and the Baghdad Railway. . . . The foreign offices of Europe were preoccupied with routine work: as the Permanent Under-Secretary in the

British Foreign Office wrote to the ambassador in Berlin in May: "You will see from the print that there is very little of interest taking place at this moment in Europe, and were it not for the troubles in Mexico we should be in comparative calm here." . . .

Accordingly, the short period between the news of the Austrian ultimatum to Serbia and the outbreak of war did not allow for much considered reflection about the implications of the crisis. "It has only needed a week to bring Europe to the eve of a catastrophe unique in history," the French business weekly *La Semaine Financière* commented on 1 August; and a young Austrian socialist wrote a few months later: "The outbreak of the war surprised and depressed us all. We may well have been previously convinced that the anarchy of the capitalist world would eventually lead to a bloody clash between the European powers, but the moment of catastrophe found us completely unprepared." Just as in studying the actions of the politicians and diplomats, we have the impression that they were repeatedly being overtaken by events, so too the public had little time or opportunity to grasp what was happening. This is one of the reasons for the collapse of the movement against the war which had been a prominent feature of pre-war politics and which had been taken very seriously by the governments of those countries such as Germany and France where it appeared to be the strongest. . . .

In the short term, governments were very successful in convincing their citizens that they were the victims of aggression and in appealing to immediate feelings of patriotism and self-preservation which proved stronger than any internationalist convictions. . . . The fact, too, that mobilization in each country proceeded without a hitch showed how strong the sense of discipline and patriotism was which the conscripts had acquired during their period of military service. . . . Once mobilization had been declared and men had actually left for the front, any agitation against war could easily seem an act of betrayal not of an abstract fatherland but of one's own party comrades. One socialist member of the Reichstag remembered that just before leaving for Berlin and the vote on the war credits, a reservist said to him, "You are going to Berlin, to the Reichstag: think of us here: see to it that we have all we need: don't be stingy in voting money."

The Austrian socialist politicians had much the same experience, faced with the popular mood in Vienna which, as the British ambassador noted, on receipt of the news of the breach of relations with Serbia "burst into a frenzy of delight, vast crowds parading the streets and singing patriotic songs till the small hours of the morning." Victor Adler, the internationally respected leader of the Social Democratic Party, shocked his colleagues at the meeting of the International Socialist Bureau by declaring: "The party is defenseless. . . . Demonstrations in support of the war are taking place in the streets." . . . In Hungary . . . all other parties were agreed on sinking their differences and unanimous in their enthusiastic support for the war.

The experiences in the other capitals of Europe were similar. In Russia the five Bolshevik members of the Duma did indeed vote against the war credits (and were later arrested) while the other socialists abstained. But these at the time were very small gestures compared with the enthusiasm for war expressed at least by the articulate members of Russian society; and there were people on the Left ready to support the war. The old anarchist leader, Prince Peter Kropotkin, . . . was soon urging the Russians to "defend themselves like wild beasts" against the Germans "fighting like devils and trampling on all the rules of humanity."

In Britain, a country without conscription, the immediate effects of mobilization were less dramatic and widespread than in the continental countries. . . . But the opposition to war dwindled fast. . . . Bertrand Russell, looking back on August 1914 and perhaps conscious of the courage which it had taken to swim against the stream in wartime, remembered: "I spent the evening [of 3 August] walking round the streets, especially in the neighbourhood of Trafalgar Square, noticing cheering crowds, and making myself sensitive to the emotions of passers-by. During this and the following days I discovered to my amazement that average men and women were delighted at the prospect of war."

For all the misgivings and anxiety which many in all countries of Europe must have felt, there is enough evidence of widespread enthusiasm especially among the more articulate members of society to suggest that the mood with which war was received was often one of excitement and relief. . . . It is certain that for a brief period in August 1914, to which some men were always to look back as one of the great moments of their lives, war made people forget their differences and created a sense of national unity in each country, so that in French villages the curé and the schoolteacher spoke to each other for the first time and in the Reichstag in Berlin socialist deputies attended the Kaiser's reception. . . . The acceptance of war when it came was the result of decades in which patriotism had been inculcated at many levels of national life all over Europe. It was also the result of years in which international relations had been discussed in the neo-Darwinian language of the struggle for survival and the survival of the fittest, and in which ideas of liberation through violence, whether for personal or national emancipation, had become common. The mood of 1914 must be seen partly as the product of a widespread revolt against the liberal values of peace and rational solutions of all problems which had been taken for granted by many people for much of the nineteenth century. . . . Certainly the young men who went off with such enthusiasm to fight in the first campaigns of the war were full of ideas of the desirability of war as a liberating experience and as the means of achieving a new national solidarity. . . .

We must also look elsewhere for the origins of the patriotic instincts which produced the acceptance, often with enthusiasm, of the call to arms in 1914. . . . The reactions of ordinary people in the crisis of 1914 were the result of the history they had learnt at school, the stories about the national past which they had been told as children and an instinctive sense of loyalty and solidarity with their neighbours and workmates. In each country children were taught the duties of patriotism and the glory of past national achievements. . . . A passage from a popular manual of French history for schools, republished and revised in 1912, is surely not very different in sentiment from similar textbooks in use in Germany or Britain: "War is not probable, but it is possible. It is for that reason that France remains armed and always ready to defend itself. . . . In defending France we are defending the land where we were born, the most beautiful and the most bountiful country in the world." . . .

Few of the people who talked of war had a very clear picture of what the war would be like; and very few indeed foresaw anything like what the war actually became. . . . In England there were recurrent panics about "a bolt from the blue," a sudden attack by the German fleet on the coast of Britain as a preliminary to an invasion; and in Germany the blustering and indiscreet language of the British First Sea Lord, Admiral Sir John Fisher, contributed to a fear that the British navy might make a sudden strike at a German navy base — a fear sufficient in 1907 to make parents in Kiel keep their children away from school for two days because "Der Fischer kommt.". . .

By 1914 the idea, if not the reality, of war was familiar. Each international crisis from 1905 on seemed to bring it near, although each time war was avoided there were always optimists who thought this would always happen. . . . Yet for many people war was not considered as a wholly undesirable experience: some saw it as a solution to social and political problems, a necessary surgery to make the body politic whole: others saw it as an opportunity to escape from the routine and tedium of their ordinary lives, a great adventure or a sporting challenge. A few saw it as an opportunity for revolution, as, to use Lenin's phrase, a "great accelerator." . . .

Those political leaders who took the decision to go to war had a sense of the overriding importance of preserving what were regarded as vital national interests. . . . When the decision to go to war was taken, governments were able to fight the war because their subjects accepted the necessity for it. To most people war appeared, or was presented, as an inescapable necessity if they were to preserve their country and their homes from foreign invasion; and they did not question what they had heard for generations about the glories and superior qualities of their own nation.

Michael Howard

Europe on the Eve of the First World War

Michael Howard, for many years Regius Professor at Oxford University and until recently of Yale University, is best known for his many studies of modern warfare, including *The Continental Commitment, War and the Liberal Conscience,* and *The Laws of War.* In this selection, Howard analyzes the triad of statesmen, soldiers, and people on the eve of the Great War. He offers incisive comments on the statesmen and soldiers in Vienna, Berlin, St. Petersburg, Paris, and London who in July 1914 made the decisions to go to war. He argues that planners in each capital believed that they had a better-than-even chance of winning. He furthermore explains that they all felt certain that war was inevitable, that it would be short, that the best chance for victory lay in the offensive, and that armies would have to endure very heavy losses. Finally, Howard offers a few comments on the "war euphoria" of 1914.

Europe was taken by surprise by the occasion for the war — so may other, comparable crises had been successfully surmounted during the past five years — but not by the fact of it. All over the continent long-matured plans were put into action. With a really remarkable absence of confusion, millions of men reported for duty, were converted or, rather, reconverted into soldiers, and loaded into the trains which were to take them to the greatest battlefields in the history of mankind. It cannot be said that during the summer weeks of 1914, while the crisis was ripening towards its bloody solution, the peoples of Europe in general were exercising any pressure on their governments to go to war, but neither did they try to restrain them. When war did come, it was accepted almost without question; in some quarters indeed with wild demonstrations of relief.

Oxford University Press 1988. Reprinted from *The Coming of the First World War,* edited by R. J. W. Evans and Hartmut Pogge von Strandmann (1988) by permission of Oxford University Press.

The historian is faced with two distinct questions. Why did war come? And when it did come, why was it so prolonged and destructive? In the background there is a further, unanswerable question: If the political and military leaders of Europe had been able to foresee that prolongation and that destruction, would the war have occurred at all? Everyone, naturally, went to war in the expectation of victory, but might they have felt that at such a cost even victory was not worthwhile? That is the kind of hypothetical question which laymen put and historians cannot answer. But we can ask another and less impossible question: What did the governments of Europe think would happen to them if they did *not* go to war? Why did war, with all its terrible uncertainties, appear to them as a preferable alternative to remaining at peace?

Clausewitz described war as being compounded of a paradoxical trinity: the governments for which it was an instrument of policy; the military for whom it was the exercise of a skill; and the people as a whole, the extent of whose involvement determined the intensity with which the war would be waged, This functional distinction is of course an oversimplification. In all the major states of Europe military and political leaders shared a common attitude and cultural background, which shaped their perceptions and guided their judgments. The same emotions which inspired peoples were likely also to affect their political and military leaders; and those emotions could be shaped by propaganda, by education, and by the socialization process to which so much of the male population of continental Europe had been subject through four decades of at least two years' compulsory military service at a highly impressionable age (though it must be noted that the British, who were not subjected to the same treatment, reacted no differently from their continental neighbours to the onset and continuation of the war). Still, the triad of government, military, and public opinion provides a useful framework for analysis, and one that I shall use for the remainder of this [selection].

First, the governments. Although none of them could foresee the full extent of the ordeal which lay before them, no responsible statesman, even in Germany, believed that they were in for "a fresh, jolly little war." It was perhaps only when they had taken their irrevocable decisions that the real magnitude of the risks which they were running came fully home to them, but that is a very common human experience. Bethmann Hollweg in particular saw the political dangers with gloomy clarity: a world war, he warned the Bavarian minister, "would topple many a throne." There had indeed been a certain amount of wild writing and speaking over the past ten years, especially in Germany, about the value of war as a panacea for social ills; and the remarkable way in which social and political differences did disappear the moment war was declared has tempted some historians to assume that this effect was foreseen and therefore intended: that the opportunity was deliberately seized by the Asquith Cabinet, for example, to distract attention from the intractable Irish problem to continental adventures, or that the German imperial government saw it as a chance to settle the hash of the Social Democrats for good. One can only say that minute scrutiny of the material by, now, several generations of historians has failed to produce any serious evidence to support this view.

Rather, the opposite was the case: governments were far from certain how their populations would react to the coming of war, and how they would stand up to its rigours. A whole generation of English publicists had been stressing the social consequences of even a temporary blockade of the British Isles: soaring insurance rates, unemployment, bread-riots, revolution. The French army, for ten years past the butt of left-wing agitation, was gloomy about the prospects of anything like an enthusiastic response from the conscripts recalled to the colours, and the French security services stood by to arrest left-wing leaders at the slightest sign of trouble. It was only with the greatest reluctance that the German army enforced military service on the supposedly unreliable population of the industrial regions. The Russian government had within the past ten years seen one war end in revolution, and for at least some of its members this seemed good reason to keep out of another. It was one thing to enhance the prestige of the government and undermine support for its domestic enemies by conducting a strong forward policy, whether in Morocco or in the Balkans. It was another to subject the fragile consensus and dubious loyalties of societies so torn by class and national conflict as were the states of Europe in 1914 to the terrible strain of a great war. Governments did so only on the assumption, spoken or unspoken, that that war, however terrible, would at least be comparatively short; no longer, probably, than the six months which had seen out the last great war in Europe in 1870. How could it be otherwise? A prolonged war of attrition, as Count Schlieffen had pointed out in a famous article in 1909, could not be conducted when it required the expenditure of milliards to sustain armies numbered in millions. The only person in any position of responsibility who appears to have thought differently was Lord Kitchener: a British imperial soldier who had served outside Europe throughout his career and who had never, so far as we know, seriously studied the question at all.

But whether the war was short or long, it was for all governments a leap into a terrible dark, and the penalties for defeat were likely to be far greater than the traditional ones of financial indemnities and territorial loss. So we come back to the question: What appeared to be the alternatives? And in the event of victory, what appeared the probable gains? Why, in the last resort, did the governments of Europe prefer the terrifying uncertainties of war to the prospect of no war?

Let us begin where the war itself effectively began, in Vienna. Was not the prospect which lay before the statesmen of Vienna, even if this crisis were successfully "managed," one of continuous frustration abroad and disintegration at home? Of a Serbia, doubled in size after the Balkan Wars, ever more boldly backing the claims of the Bosnian irredentists, while the South Slavs agitated with ever greater confidence for an autonomy that the Magyars would never permit them to exercise? What serious prospect was there of the Empire hanging together once the old Emperor had gone? A final settling of accounts with Serbia while Germany held the Russians in check must have appeared the only chance of saving the Monarchy, whatever Berlin might say; and with a blank cheque from Berlin, Vienna could surely face the future with a greater confidence than had been felt there for very many years. No wonder Berchtold and his colleagues took their time in drafting their ultimatum: they must have found the process highly enjoyable. A successful war would put the Monarchy back in business again, and keep it there for many years to come.

What about the government in Berlin? Was this the moment it had been waiting for ever since the famous Council of War in December 1912? . . . But if one again asks the questions, what the imperial German government had to lose by peace and gain by war, the answers seem very clear. One of the things it had to lose by peace was its Austrian ally, which would become an increasingly useless makeweight as it grew ever less capable of solving its internal problems or protecting its own (and German) interests in the Balkans against the encroachments of Russia and Russia's protégés. Another was Germany's capacity to hold her own against a Dual Alliance in which French capital was building up a Russian army whose future size and mobility appeared far beyond the capacity of any German force to contain. It would not be too anachronistic to suggest that the shadow of Russia's future status as a superpower was already rendering out of date all calculations based on the traditional concept of a European balance. If war was to come at all — and few people in the imperial government doubted that it would — then it was self-evidently better to have it now, while there was still a fair chance of victory. By 1917, when the Russians had completed the Great Programme of rearmament and railway building which they had begun, with French funding, in 1912, it might be too late.

And, for Germany, there was a lot to be gained by war. The domination of the Balkans and perhaps the Middle East; the final reduction of France to a position from which she could never again, even with allies, pose a military threat to German power; the establishment of a position on the Continent that would enable her to compete on equal terms with England and attain the grandiose if ill-defined status of a world power: all this, in July 1914, must have appeared perfectly feasible. In September, when the Programme of her war aims was drafted, it looked as if it had almost been achieved. Even in a less bellicose and more self-confident society than Wilhelmine Germany, the opportunity might have appeared too good to miss.

In Vienna and Berlin then, there seemed much to be lost by peace and gained by war. In St. Petersburg, the ambitions for Balkan expansion and the "recovery" of Constantinople, checked in 1878 and 1885, were far from dead, but they can hardly by counted a major element in Russian political calculations in July 1914. More serious were the costs of remaining at peace: abandoning Serbia and all the gains of the past five years; facing the wrath of the pan-Slavs in the Duma and their French allies; and watching the Central Powers establish and consolidate an unchallengeable dominance in south-east Europe. Even so, these costs were hardly irredeemable.

Russia had been humiliated before in the Balkans and been able to restore her authority. She had no vital interests there which, once lost, could never be recovered. Above all, she had nothing to lose, in terms of military power, by waiting, and a great deal to gain. Of all the major powers, Russia's entry into the war can be categorized as the least calculated, the most unwise, and ultimately of course the most disastrous.

As for Paris and London, a successful war would certainly remove — as it ultimately did — a major threat to their security. But the advantages to be gained by war did not enter into their calculations, whereas the perils of remaining at peace quite evidently did. The French government took little comfort from the long-term advantages to be gained from the growth of Russian military power and the consequent advisability of postponing the issue until 1917. It was more conscious of its immediate weakness confronted by the growing numbers of the German army. In 1914, after the increase of the past two years, the German peacetime strength had reached 800,000 men, the wartime strength 3.8 million. Thanks to their new and controversial Three-Year Law, the French could match this with 700,000 men in peace, 3.5 million in war. But with a population only 60 per cent of the German, that was almost literally their final throw. Completion of the Russian reforms was three long years away. In the long run Russian strength might redress the balance, but in the long run a large number of Frenchmen could be dead and their nation reduced to the status of Italy or Spain. So the French government saw no reason to urge caution on St. Petersburg, and even less reason to refrain from supporting its ally when Germany declared war on her on 1 August.

For the British government, composed as it was very largely (though by no means entirely) of men to whom the whole idea of war was antipathetic and who were responsible to a parliamentary party deeply suspicious of militarism and of continental involvement, there appeared nothing to be gained by war, and perhaps more than any of its continental equivalents it was conscious of the possible costs. But it was equally conscious of the cost of remaining at peace. Britain would not be the *tertius gaudens* in a continental war. She had no demands to make on any of the belligerents, no territorial aspirations, no expectation of economic gain. So far as the British government was concerned, Norman Angell's famous book

The Great Illusion was preaching to the converted. But if the Dual Alliance defeated Germany unaided Britain would be, for the two victors, an object of hostility and contempt. All the perils of imperial rivalry temporarily dispersed by the Entente with France of 1904 and the accords with Russia of 1907 would reappear. If, on the other hand, Germany won and established a continental hegemony, Britain would face a threat to her security unknown since the days of Napoleon. Leaving any consideration of honour, sentiment, or respect for treaties on one side — and let us remember that that generation of Englishmen did *not* leave them on one side but regarded them as quite central — every consideration of *realpolitik* dictated that Britain, having done her best to avert the war, should enter it on the side of France and Russia once it began.

When the statesmen of Europe declared war in 1914, they all shared one common assumption: that they had a better-than-evens chance of winning it. In making this assumption they relied on their military advisers; so it is now time to look at the second element in our triad: the soldiers.

The first thing to note about the soldiers, certainly those of western Europe, is that they were professionals; most of them professionals of a very high order. Those of them who were well-born or aspired to that status certainly shared all the feudal value-system so excoriated by Professor Arno Mayer in his work on *The Persistence of the Old Regime*. Those who were not probably had more than their fair share of the prevalent philosophy of Social Darwinism and regarded war, not as an unpleasant necessity, but as a test of manhood and of national fitness for survival. In all armies, then as now, there were incompetents who through good luck or good connections reached unsuitably high rank; but a study of the military literature of the period strongly indicates that the military, especially those responsible for the armament, training, organization, and deployment of armies, were no fools, worked hard, and took their professions very seriously indeed. And they, also, shared certain common assumptions.

The first was that war was inevitable. The now much-quoted statement made by General von Moltke at the so-called Council of War in December 1912, "I hold war to be inevitable, and the sooner the better," can be paralleled with comparable expressions by responsible figures in every army in Europe. They may have differed over the second part of the sentence — whether it was better to get it over with quickly or wait for a more favourable moment — but from 1911 onward it is hard to find any military leader suggesting that war could or should any longer by avoided. The change of mood in the summer of that year, provoked by the Agadir crisis, was very marked. In France a new political leadership appointed new military chiefs, who belatedly and desperately began to prepare their ramshackle army for the test of war. The Dual Alliance was reactivated, Russian mobilization schedules were speeded up, and the Great Programme of Russian military modernization was set on foot. In Germany the agitation began which contributed so powerfully to the massive increase in the military strength of the German army. In Britain the government gave its blessing to the army's plans for sending the British Expeditionary Force to France, and Winston Churchill was sent to the Admiralty to bring the navy into line. The extent to which war was generally regarded as inevitable or desirable by the public as a whole is still difficult to gauge — though if the "distant drummer" penetrated into the summer idylls of A.E. Housman it is reasonable to suppose that less remote figures found the sound pretty deafening. But certainly for the military the evidence is overwhelming that the question in their mind was not "whether" but "when." They saw their job as being, not to deter war, but to fight it.

The second assumption, which they shared with the statesmen they served, was that the war would be short. It requires quite exceptional perspicacity to visualize anything else. Ivan Bloch in his work *La Guerre future*, published in 1898, had forecast with amazing accuracy how the power of modern weapons would produce deadlock on the battlefield and how the resulting attrition would destroy the fabric of the belligerent societies. Bloch's thesis was widely known and much discussed in military periodicals. But since he was in effect saying that the military were now faced with a problem which they could not solve, it was not to be expected that many soldiers would agree with him. As for his conclusion, that war in the future would be, if not impossible, then certainly suicidal, it had already been shown not to be true.

In 1904–5 Russian and Japan had fought a war with all the weapons whose lethal effects were so gruesomely described by Bloch, and Japan had won a clear-cut victory which established her in the ranks of the major powers. The effect on Russia had been much as Bloch had described, but revolution and defeat always stalked hand in hand. The war had indeed lasted for well over a year, but it had been fought by both belligerents at the end of long and difficult supply lines. In Europe, where communications were plentiful and short, and armies at hair-trigger readiness, the pattern of the German wars of unification seemed much more relevant: rapid mobilization and deployment of all available forces, a few gigantic battles — battles, indeed, which might be prolonged for days if not weeks as the protagonists probed for a flank or a weak point in the enemy defences — and a decision within a matter of months. Because that decision would be reached so quickly, it was important that all forces should be committed to action. There was no point in bringing up reserves after the battle had been lost. There was even less point — if indeed it occurred to anyone to do so — to prepare an industrial base to sustain a war of *matériel* which might last for years. The idea that any national economy could endure such an ordeal was self-evidently absurd.

This shared assumption — that the war would inevitably be short — led on to another: that the best chances of victory lay in immediately taking the offensive. With the wisdom of hindsight it is easy for subsequent generations to condemn the suicidal unreality of this idea, but in the circumstances of the time it appeared reasonable enough. An offensive gave the best hope of disrupting or preempting the mobilization of the opponent and bringing him to battle under favourable conditions. As in a wrestling-match which had to be settled in a matter of minutes, to yield the initiative was to court defeat. The French had stood on the defensive in 1870 and been defeated. The Russians had stood on the defensive in 1904–5 and been defeated. Those who had studied the history of the American Civil War, who included all students of the British Army Staff College at Camberley, knew that the only hope of a Confederate victory had lain in a successful offensive, and that once Lee passed over to the defensive after the Battle of Gettysburg his defeat was only a matter of time. The lessons of history seemed to reinforce the strategic imperatives of 1914.

And let us not forget what those strategic imperatives were. The Germans had to destroy the French power of resistance before the full force of Russian strength could be developed. The Russians had to attack sufficiently early, and in sufficient strength, to take the weight off the French. The Austrians had to attack the Russians in order to take the weight off the Germans. For the French alone a defensive strategy was in theory feasible, but the precedent of 1870 made it understandably unpopular, and the national mood made it inconceivable. The doctrine of the offensive was certainly carried, in the pre-1914 French army, to quite unreasonable lengths, but that does not in itself mean that a posture of defence would necessarily have been any more effective in checking the German advance in 1914 than it was in 1940.

Finally we must remember that the stalemate on the western front did not develop for six months, and that on the eastern front it never developed at all. The open warfare of manoeuvre for which the armies of Europe had prepared was precisely what, in the autumn of 1914, they got. It resulted in eastern Europe in a succession of spectacular German victories, and given bolder and more flexible leadership it might very well have done the same in the West. The terrible losses suffered by the French in Alsace in August and by the British and Germans in Flanders in November came in encounter battles, not in set-piece assaults against prepared defensive positions; and they were losses which, to the military leadership at least, came as no great surprise.

For this was the final assumption shared by soldiers throughout Europe: in any future war, armies would have to endure very heavy losses indeed. The German army, for one, had never forgotten the price it paid for its victories in 1870, when the French had been armed with breech-loading rifles which in comparison with the weapons now available were primitive. Since then the effects of every new weapon had been studied with meticulous care, and no professional soldier was under any illusions about the damage that would be caused; not simply by machine-guns (which were in fact seen as ideal weapons of a mobile offensive), but by magazine-loading rifles and by quick-firing artillery firing shrapnel at infantry in the open and high explosives against trenches. Their effects had been studied not only through controlled experiment, but in action, in the South African and Russo-Japanese Wars. The conclusion generally drawn was that in future infantry would be able to advance only in open formations, making use of all available cover, under the protection of concentrated artillery fire.

But whatever precautions they took, sooner or later troops would have to assault across open ground with the bayonet, and they must then be prepared to take very heavy losses. This had happened in Manchuria, where the Japanese were generally seen as having owed their success not simply to their professional skills, but to their contempt for death. European Social Darwinians gravely propounded the terrible paradox, that a nation's fitness to survive depended on the readiness of its individual members to die. Avoidance of casualties was seen as no part of the general's trade, and willingness to accept them was regarded as a necessity for commander and commanded alike. Into the literature of pre-war Europe there crept the word which was to become the terrible leitmotiv of the coming conflict: "sacrifice"; more particularly, "the supreme sacrifice."

That may have been all very well for professional soldiers whose job it is, after all, to die for their country if they cannot arrange matters any less wastefully. But the people who were going to die in the next war were not going to be just the professional soldiers. They would be the People: men recalled to the coulours from civilian life or, in the case of England, volunteering to "do their bit." Would these young men, enervated by urban living, rotted by socialist propaganda, show the same Bushido spirit as the Japanese? This question was constantly propounded in military and right-wing literature during the ten years before the war. Kipling for one, surveying the civilians of Edwardian England in the aftermath of the Boer War, very much doubted it, and taunted his fellow countrymen in a series of scornful philippics:

> *Fenced by your careful fathers, ringed by your leaden seas,*
> *Long did ye wake in quiet and long lie down at ease;*
> *Till ye said of Strife, "What is it"? of the Sword.*
> > *"It is far from our ken";*
> *Till ye made a sport of your shrunken hosts and a toy*
> > *of your armèd men.*

In Germany Heinrich Class and Friedrich von Bernhardi, in France Charles Maurras and Charles Péguy expressed the same doubts about the capacity of their peoples to rise to the level of the forthcoming test. But the astonishing thing was that, when the time came, they did so rise. Why?

This brings us belatedly to the third element in the triad, the People. Without the support, or at least the acquiescence of the peoples of Europe, there would have been no war. This is the most interesting and most complex area for historians to investigate. We know a lot — almost to excess— about the mood of the intellectuals and the élites in 1914, but what about the rest? There are now some excellent studies of local and popular reactions in Britain, largely based on the superb sources at the Imperial War Museum. M. Jean-Jacques Becker had done path-breaking work for France in his study *1914: Comment les Français sont entrés dans la guerre* (Paris, 1977) but elsewhere there remains much research to be done or, where done, brought together. My own ignorance forces me to treat this vast subject briefly and impressionistically, and I hope that others will be able to correct some of my misconceptions and fill some of the yawning gaps.

What does appear self-evident is that the doubts which European leaders felt about the morale of their peoples proved in 1914 to be ill-founded. Those who welcomed war with enthusiasm may have been a minority concentrated in the big cities, but those who opposed it were probably a smaller minority still. The vast majority were willing to do what their governments expected of them. Nationalistically oriented public education; military service which, however unwelcome and tedious, bred a sense of cohesion and national identity; continuing habits of social deference: all this helps explain, at a deeper level than does the strident propaganda of the popular press, why the populations of Europe responded so readily to the call when it came. For the "city-bred populations" so mistrusted by right-wing politicians the war came as an adventure, an escape from humdrum or intolerable lives into a world of adventure and comradeship. Among the peasants of France, as M. Becker has shown us, there was little enthusiasm, but rather glum acceptance of yet another unavoidable hardship in lives which were and always had been unavoidably hard; but the hardship fell as much on those who were left behind as on those who went away. The same can no doubt be said of the peasants of central and eastern Europe as well.

There was probably only a tiny minority, also, which considered the idea of war in itself repellent. Few military historians, and no popular historians, had ever depicted the realities of the battlefield in their full horror, and only a few alarmist prophets could begin to conceive what the realities of future battlefields would be like. Their nations, so the peoples of Europe had learned at school, had achieved their present greatness through successful wars — the centenaries of the battles of Trafalgar and of Leipzig had recently been celebrated with great enthusiasm in Britain and Germany — and there was no reason to think that they would not one day have to fight again. Military leaders were everywhere respected and popular figures (Kitchener and Roberts more so, probably, than Balfour and Asquith); military music was an intrinsic part of popular culture. In the popular mind, as in the military mind, wars were seen not as terrible evils to be deterred, but as necessary struggles to be fought and won.

I have touched on the Social Darwinism of the period: the view, so widespread among intellectuals and publicists as well as among soldiers, that struggle was a natural process of development in the social as in the natural order of the world, and war a necessary procedure for ensuring survival of the fittest, among nations as among species. It is hard to know how seriously to take this. Its manifestations catch the eye of a contemporary historian if only because they are, to our generation, so very shocking. But how widely were such views really held, and how far were people like F. N. Maude, Sidney Low, or Benjamin Kidd generally regarded as cranks? The same applies to the much-touted influence of Nietzsche and of Bergson among intellectuals — the creed of liberation from old social norms, of heroic egotism, of action as a value transcending all others. How widespread was their influence? Did it make the idea of war more generally acceptable than it otherwise would have been? Intellectuals, I am afraid, tend to overrate the importance of other intellectuals, or at best attribute to them an influence which becomes important only among later generations. Webern and Schoenberg may have been composing in pre-war Vienna, but the tunes which rang in the ears of the 1914 generation were those of Franz Lehár and Richard Strauss.

And if there was a "War Movement," there was also, far more evident and purposeful, a Peace Movement, derived from older liberal-rationalist roots. It was stronger in some countries than in others; then as now, it flourished more successfully in Protestant than in Catholic cultures, at its strongest in Scandinavia, the Netherlands, and Britain (not to mention the United States), weakest in Italy and Spain. It was indeed the apparent strength and influence of the Peace Movement, especially at the time of The Hague Conferences, that provoked so much of the polemical writings of the Social Darwinians and caused so much concern to nationalistic politicians. In imperial Germany the Peace Movement had an uphill struggle; but if Heinrich Class and the Pan-German League were thundering out the dogmas of the War Movement, the far larger and more important Social Democratic Party rejected them — as did the overwhelmingly dominant Liberal-Labour coalition in England and the left wing led by Jean Jaurès which triumphed at the polls in France in the spring of 1914. Social Darwinsim may have been not so much the prevailing *Zeitgeist* as a sharp minority reaction against a much stronger and deeply rooted liberal, rational, and progressive creed whose growing influence seemed to some to be undermining the continuing capacity of nations to defend themselves.

But the events of 1914 showed these right-wing fears to be misplaced. Everywhere the leaders of the Peace Movement found themselves isolated: small and increasingly unpopular minorities of idealists, intellectuals, and religious zealots. Events made it clear that, whatever their influence among intellectuals and élites, both the Peace and the War Movements were marginal to the attitudes of the peoples of Europe. Those peoples did *not* reject war. Nor did they regard it as the highest good, the fulfillment of human destiny. They accepted it as a fact of life. They trusted their rulers and marched when they were told. Many did so with real enthusiasm; perhaps the more highly educated they were, the greater the enthusiasm they felt. None knew what they were marching towards, and any romantic notions they had about war shredded to pieces the moment they came under artillery fire. But they adjusted to the ordeal with astonishing speed and stoicism. It was indeed because they adjusted so well that the ordeal lasted for as long as it did.

L. L. Farrar, Jr.

The Short-War Illusion

Lancelot Farrar, professor of history formerly of Lewis and Clark College, offers yet another insight into the "mood of 1914." Specifically, Farrar suggests that the major European powers were willing to accept war partly because of their certainty that the conflict would be short, a quick, "cleansing thunderstorm," as Winston Churchill put it. The nature of the European alliance system, however, prompted most of the continental powers, especially Austria-Hungary and France, to risk protracted war in the face of possible political collapse.

The behavior of the great powers during the early months of the war can therefore be understood in terms of their prewar policies. These policies collided during the July crisis when each sought diplomatic victory, and, under the circumstances, a diplomatic victory for one power would have required a diplomatic defeat for another. Since none of the powers were willing to accept diplomatic defeat, all chose war as a less undesirable alternative. There were, however, other more positive reasons for electing war as far as Berlin, Vienna, Paris, St. Petersburg, and Belgrade were concerned (these views were probably not shared in London and certainly were not in Brussels). War seemed to be a means of achieving the objectives which eluded diplomacy. By choosing war Germany sought to shore up its alliance with Austria-Hungary and to shatter the Anglo-Franco-Russian alliance. Similarly, war was a means by which Austria-Hungary might preserve itself and increase its influence in the Balkans. Russia was anxious to preserve its alliance with France and to dominate the Balkans. France desired to preserve itself and the alliance with Russia and to resuscitate its great power status. Only Britain wanted to maintain the *status quo* which served British interests. All the continental powers probably also entertained more ambitious objectives

Permission granted to use text from *The Short-War Illusion: German Policy, Strategy and Domestic Affairs, August–December 1914*, by L. L. Farrar, Jr., published by ABC-Clio, 1973, pp. 4–11, footnotes omitted.

which would have fundamentally altered the state system. But none of the powers specifically sought war to destroy the system, and each envisaged what it perceived as reconstruction rather than resolution. Thus, the prewar ends remained basically the same, but the means were changed from diplomacy to war. War seemed merely policy by other means.

The approaching war was perceived in this way because of the prevailing view that it would be short. Even more significant than the prevalence of the short-war view was the fact that those who expected a long war did little to prepare for it. Their inaction was due to the widespread assumption that the state of Europe's political and economic development made such preparations either unnecessary or impossible.

The assumption of a short war dominated German strategy. It had not always been so. Bismarck's Chief of the General Staff Helmuth von Moltke predicted that the war would last seven or even thirty years. At the other end of the political spectrum, Friedrich Engels shared this view, though he estimated more accurately — three or four years. The turning point in German strategic thinking occurred with Moltke's second successor, Alfred von Schlieffen, who assumed that a lengthy conflict was impossible "in an age in which the existence of nations is based on the uninterrupted progress of trade and commerce. . . . A strategy of exhaustion is impossible when the maintenance of millions necessitates the expenditure of billions." Schlieffen's successor, Moltke's nephew Helmuth von Moltke, was characteristically ambivalent; sometimes he predicted a long, sometimes a short war. Regardless of his varied predictions, his strategy remained constant — he planned a short war. The short-war assumption was apparently shared by most of the German officer corps and was implied in prewar discussions about the possibility of a preventive war. Germany's initial military successes during the first weeks of the war seemed to confirm the assumption. Though shaken by the Marne setback in September, that assumption was revived during October only to be shattered by the end of 1914.

The same assumption underlay German diplomacy. Chancellor Theobald von Bethmann Hollweg reportedly predicted that the war would be a "brief storm." The Kaiser and court seem to have shared this view. The government's discussion of war aims was based on the expectation that France would be defeated quickly and that England would resign itself to French defeat. Despite fluctuation, this assumption remained the basis of German diplomacy until the end of 1914.

To the extent that they expressed themselves, German financiers and industrialists probably shared the short-war assumption because of the government's statements. Although Schlieffen justified his short-war assumption in economic and political terms, he virtually ignored these considerations in his planning for war, as did his successor, the younger Moltke. Some effort was made on the eve of war to foresee the economic implication of a conflict, but little was accomplished, due to bureaucratic inertia and because it was assumed that a short war would make preparations unnecessary. Consistent with this assumption, factories and farms were subordinated to the military front — industrial and agricultural workers were drafted as the war began. A few industrialists and financiers doubted that the war would be short, in particular, that England would accept a French defeat. But most seem to have expected the conflict to end quickly, indeed, perhaps too quickly, and even agitated against "premature peace."

German politicians, leaders of the Bundesstaaten, and the masses apparently shared these views. Those conservatives who felt that war would reinforce the domestic *status quo* assumed that the conflict would be short and successful. This opinion was echoed by at least one Socialist member of the Reichstag. Other members of the Reichstag considered a long war to be economically infeasible. The unanimous acceptance of the domestic political truce declared in August was justified by the anticipation that it would be temporary; politics were to resume when the Reichstag reconvened in December following a German victory. This view was encouraged by the Kaiser's assurance that victory would be won "before the leaves fall." The assumed brevity of the war caused the government and leftist politicians to discuss postwar problems in September and October. The demands from leaders of several Bundesstaaten for war aims were prompted by an expectation of imminent victory. Since the government assumed that the masses expected a short war, it concealed German military setbacks, and Bethmann considered not attending the Reichstag in December.

Austro-Hungarian leaders evidently shared the assumption. Franz Conrad von Hötzendorf, the Austro-Hungarian Chief of the

General Staff, repeatedly demanded a preventive war. The hopes of Leopold von Berchtold, the Austro-Hungarian Foreign Minister, and others for a rapid punitive expedition against Serbia were based on the short-war assumption. Hungarian Minister President Stephan Tisza was ambivalent; he expected an Austro-Hungarian attack on Serbia to be successful but feared that it might precipitate a protracted European conflict.

British leaders generally seem to have assumed that the war would be short. Anglo-French strategic discussions during the prewar decade focused on the question of how quickly and where British troops should be sent to aid the French, since the critical battles would presumably be fought early. When war broke out, those who had dominated these discussions persuaded the cabinet to send British troops quickly. But this decision was opposed by Lord Kitchener, Secretary of State for War, who did not participate in the prewar discussions and expected the war to last several years. Foreign Secretary Edward Grey's attitude was unclear; his disinclination to send troops to the continent indicated that he expected a short war, but his oft-quoted remark about the lights going out implied a destructive and thus long war. Members of the British cabinet were shocked by Kitchener's prediction of a long conflict but nonetheless accepted it. The British financial community shared writer Norman Angell's prediction that war would destroy the European financial structure and thus could not last long.

French leaders likewise expected a short war. The French General Staff assumed it and French strategy implied it. Chief of the General Staff Joseph Joffre predicted that the coming war would be long, but his emphasis on speed and optimism at the beginning of the war suggested the opposite; most importantly, he made no preparation for a long conflict. Despite the French setbacks during August 1914, some French generals — notably Ferdinand Foch — predicted (in September) that the war was "virtually ended." The French government and politicians apparently shared his expectation.

The same assumption was reflected in the Russian strategy. The Turkish, Italian and Bulgarian governments expected a rapid German victory. The Japanese government grabbed German colonies in Asia while Germany was engaged in Europe, in part because they probably shared the short-war assumption. American observers were ambivalent; some expected a rapid German victory, while others foresaw a protracted struggle ending in German defeat.

The short-war assumption was related to policy objectives which were initially projected as reformist rather than revolutionary. A short, successful war was necessary to achieve these goals, whereas a long war — even if successful — might become revolutionary and preclude them. Consequently, the assumption of a short war was a precondition of the decision to pursue prewar objectives by war rather than diplomacy. In this sense, the desire was father to the belief. The belief that the war would be short permeated strategy, diplomacy and domestic politics during the first months of the war. It proved to be the war's greatest illusion.

Encirclement Versus Breakthrough: The Military Plans

All military plans are forward looking since they prescribe future action; conversely, actions based on plans are retrospective. During the early months of the war military strategies were based on prewar assumptions and aspirations.

The German strategic blueprint, the Schlieffen plan, was based on the assumption that Germany and Austria-Hungary would go to war against Russia, France and probably Great Britain. The German objective was victory, not mere survival. Germany could win only if the war was short, which was possible only if the enemy forces were rapidly encircled and annihilated. The annihilation of enemy forces depended upon the superiority of German forces and room to maneuver. The relative speeds of mobilization and space factors rendered French forces more susceptible to encirclement than the Russian army. Schlieffen thus decided to concentrate German forces on his northern flank facing France and to reduce German forces both on the French southern front and on the eastern front facing Russia. The consequent risks seemed congruent with the assumption that victory depended upon a short war, i.e., short-term security on all fronts might lessen the chance for rapid success and thus risk long-term failure. . . .

French decisions were probably determined primarily on the basis of political, rather than military, considerations, but military events were nonetheless important. German military success depended on French strategy. The revival of French self-confidence on the eve of the war encouraged the development of a strategy which paradoxically increased the probability of French defeat. The French Plan XVII, like the Schlieffen plan, was based on the assumption that victory necessitated an offensive. French strategists accordingly proposed to exploit the diversion of the main German force in Belgium in order to break through the German center. French and German strategies thus reinforced each other; they differed, however, in formulation. The Schlieffen plan stipulated an ultimate objective (i.e., annihilation of the French army), whereas Plan XVII did not. Plan XVII presumed that a French breakthrough and increasing Russian pressure on the eastern front would cause the Germans to renounce their offensive, withdraw in confusion, and surrender at the prospect of a long war. . . .

The proposed French strategy may, however, have avoided French political failure. By committing their forces to an immediate attack, the French received a Russian declaration of war against Germany and assurances of an eventual offensive on the eastern front. The French would therefore not be diplomatically isolated and would not need to surrender even if defeated on the battlefield. But an immediate French surrender following military defeat was a precondition for German success. Plan XVII's most important results were probably least expected. Designed to produce military victory, it might prevent military defeat. It assumed a short war, yet virtually assured a long one. Disastrous military strategy thus proved to be a desirable political policy. . . .

Austro-Hungarian and French interests . . . coincided since their positions were analogous in many ways. The decline of both as great powers had been accelerated by defeat at the hands of Germany, and the prospect of one-front wars further threatened their great power status. Since they could improve that status with a victory over a genuine great power, each urged its ally to concentrate against its primary protagonist. France wanted Russia to concentrate against Germany, while Austria-Hungary asked Germany to concentrate against Russia. Each minimized the other as a threat to its ally — France dismissed the Austro-Hungarian threat to Russia; Austria-Hungary depreciated the French threat to Germany. Their allies refused, however, to comply, and so each was compelled to meet its opponent virtually alone. Both nonetheless committed themselves to risky offensives in order to insure the minimal assistance proffered by their allies. These offensives risked immediate military defeat and were therefore poor strategically, but they were good policy since they insured future aid from their allies. In summary, France and Austria-Hungary sought political gains by taking military gambles.

In the last analysis, France and Austria-Hungary probably benefited more than their allies from their respective alliances. Russian and German strategies were caught in the same kind of vicious cycle in that success in both instances depended upon the immediate surrender of their main enemies after military defeat. The defeat of Austria-Hungary would have required a Russian concentration against it, just as a German concentration was needed against France to insure French defeat. Russian concentration against Austria-Hungary required that France divert Germany. A German concentration against France needed an Austro-Hungarian diversion of Russia. But French diversion of Germany was not likely without Russian assurances of future aid to France, just as Austria-Hungary required a German promise of future aid before it would divert Russia. This prospect of future aid from their allies virtually assured, however, that France and Austria-Hungary would not surrender immediately. Consequently, the German commitment to Austria- Hungary almost certainly precluded a Russian victory, whereas the Russian commitment to France significantly diminished the probability of a German victory. In each case, the preconditions for German and Russian military victory legislated against their political success. The risks of military failure taken by Austria-Hungary and France, on the other hand, may have prevented their political failure.

Logically, the situation almost precluded a short war. A short war would have ensued if the defeated powers surrendered immediately after defeat which they might have done if their alliances had collapsed, leaving them politically isolated. But if the alliance system had collapsed, there would probably have been no war. The war occurred because the alliance system continued. Since the alliance system insured that military defeat would not result in political isolation, the defeated nations would not be inclined to surrender immediately. The war was therefore likely to be long.

Arno J. Mayer

The Primacy of
Domestic Politics

Arno J. Mayer, professor emeritus of history at Princeton University, is best known for his works *Political Origins of the New Diplomacy* (1959), *Politics and Diplomacy of Peacemaking* (1967), *The Dynamics of Counter-revolution* (1967), *The Persistence of the Old Regime* (1981), and *Why Did the Heavens Darken? The Final Solution in History* (1988). In this selection, of which the first part is printed here, Mayer suggests that to understand the outbreak of the Great War we should pay attention to domestic dysfunctions and the possible effect of these prerevolutionary domestic tensions and disturbances on the diplomatic decisions of the governments.

When analyzing the origins of the Great War, diplomatic historians continue to focus on two sets of underlying and precipitant causes: those rooted in the dysfunctions of the international system and those rooted in the mistakes, miscalculations, and vagaries of the principal foreign-policy actors. These historians assume that in a multiple-state system the balancing of power is a natural and essential method of control, notwithstanding its inherent uncertainties. In other words, they do not question or criticize the balancing-of-power system or process as such. Instead, they tilt their lances at four developments that complicated, if not obstructed, its smooth operation: (1) the alliance system, which became increasingly polarized and rigidified, thereby threatening to transform any limited, local conflict into an unlimited, general war; (2) the attendant armaments race, which exacerbated mutual hostility, fear, and distrust; (3) the new military metaphysics, which inclined civilian foreign-policy actors to become increasingly responsive to the military leaders and their iron-clad timetables; and (4) public opinion, expressed and mobilized through the daily press, notably the yellow and jingoist dailies which were impatient with accommodation.

In addition to diagnosing these four dysfunctions in the balancing-of-power system or process, diplomatic historians also probe into the personal attitudes, motives, and objectives of the principal foreign-policy actors — heads of state, chief executives, foreign ministers, permanent foreign office officials, ambassadors, and military and naval officers. Not surprisingly, each major historian tends to have his favorite villain. Rather than indict entire nations, scholars tend to return verdicts against individual actors of a given nation or alliance. Three categories of charges are most commonly preferred: (1) that they made grave mistakes in diplomatic tactics; (2) that they miscalculated the responses of potential enemies; and (3) that they pursued objectives that were incompatible with the maintenance of the European equilibrium. But whatever the charge, in the last analysis their actions and judgments are said to have been warped by personal ambition, caprice, pique, or lack of backbone in the face of ruthless warmongers.

Admittedly, this framework of orthodox diplomatic history, tempered by amateur psychology, has been used to good advantage. It has served to uncover a great deal about the origins of the First World War in particular, and about the causes of international conflict in general.

Just the same, this time-honored approach has some rather grave limitations. In particular, it slides over (1) the proclivity of key foreign-policy actors to risk war in general, and preventive war in particular; (2) the degree to which they realized that any localized conflict was likely to develop into a major all-European or even world war; and (3) the extent to which they entertained recourse to external war for internal political purposes.

This third limitation stems very largely from the diplomatic historian's disposition to detach foreign policy hermetically from domestic politics; and to disconnect foreign-policy and diplomatic actors rigorously from the political and social context from which they originate and in which they operate.

Admittedly, this twofold dissociation, for analytic purposes, may not fatally handicap the study of the international politics of the relatively calm and elitist mid-eighteenth century. There seems little doubt, however, that this dual disjunction hinders the examination and understanding of foreign policy and diplomacy in such revolutionary eras as 1789 to 1815 and in such brief revolutionary spasms as 1848–1850.

This interconnection of domestic politics and foreign policy is exceptionally intense under prerevolutionary and revolutionary conditions. Characteristically, in the prewar years domestic tensions rose sharply at the same time that the international system became increasingly strained. Moreover, this symbiotic growth of domestic and international tensions occurred in that part of the world in which, for the first time in recorded history, government policies, including foreign policies, were shaped in the crucible of organized party, pressure, and interest politics.

In other words, on the eve of war the major European polities were far from quiescent; and both the making and the conduct of foreign policy had ceased to be the private preserve of an encapsulated elite free of political pressures and neutral in the explosive domestic controversies of their respective societies. Accordingly, the 50 percent increase in military spending in the five prewar years may not have been exclusively a function of mounting international distrust, insecurity, and hostility. In some measure it may also have been a by-product of the resolve by conservatives and ultraconservatives to foster their political position by rallying the citizenry around the flag; and to reduce the politically unsettling cyclical fluctuations of the capitalist economies by raising armaments expenditures. In this same connection it should be stressed that the chief villains of July–August 1914 — those foreign-policy actors whom diplomatic historians identify as having practiced reckless brinkmanship — were intimately tied in with those social, economic, and political strata that were battling either to maintain the domestic status quo or to steer an outright reactionary course.

To attenuate if not overcome the limitations of diplomatic history's conventional approach to the causes of the war its analytic framework should be recast to accommodate three aspects of the historical and immediate crisis that conditioned and precipitated hostilities in July–August 1914: (1) the dysfunctions in the international system; (2) the domestic dysfunctions in the would-be belligerent nations; and (3) the inextricable interplay between these two sets of dysfunctions.

Whereas the dysfunctions in the international system and the diplomatic rivalries among the major powers have been studied exhaustively and are well-known, the same cannot be said about the prewar domestic dysfunctions, notably about their all-European scope.

During the decade . . . the European nations experienced more than routine political and social disturbances. Even Britain, that paradigm of ordered change and constitutionalism, was approaching the threshold of civil war. Judging by the Curragh incident, Carson and the Ulster volunteers had the sympathy if not outright cooperation of influential civil and military leaders in their defiance of Parliament; and the Triple Alliance of railwaymen, miners, and transport workers, among whom militant syndicalists were ascendant, threatened a paralyzing general strike in case their minimum demands were not met by the fall of 1914. . . . The resulting polarization, along with the shift from debate in Westminster to direct action in the streets, eroded the vital center so essential for the politics of compromise and accommodation. Indeed, historians have wondered whether if external war had not come in 1914 England might not have been caught up in civil strife, with fatal damage to her time-honored parliamentary system.

In France, meanwhile, the struggle between the right and the left raged with unabated intensity around the twin issues of the three-year draft and the progressive income tax. As in England, the center of the political spectrum, which in France was multi-party in nature, was being eroded in favor of the two opposing extremes. . . . In Italy prewar political and labor disturbances culminated in the explosive Red Week of early June 1914. Especially once this strike wave subsided . . . the Italian middle-class nationalists assumed a position of intransigent hostility to the left — including the moderate left — which in 1915 took the form of taking Italy into the war against the will of the vast majority of the Italian nation.

As for Germany's semi-parliamentary system, which was the privileged preserve of conservative nationalists, it was heavily besieged by those parties . . . that denounced Prussia's three-class franchise and clamored for the cabinet's subordination to the Reichstag. . . . According to Arthur Rosenberg, the political and social tensions in prewar Germany were "typical of a pre-revolutionary period," and if Germany had not gone to war in 1914 "the conflict between the Imperial Government and the majority of the German nation would have continued to intensify to a point at which a revolutionary situation would have been created."

The power elites in both halves of the Dual Monarchy faced increasingly explosive nationalistic unrest which, in itself, was an expression of spiraling political, economic, and social dysfunctions. Both Otto Bauer and Victor Bibl have argued convincingly that fear of southern Slav insurgency and of intensifying Austro-Czech tensions drove Vienna's political class into trying to overcome its permanent internal crisis by recourse to external war.

Simultaneously the Russian government, firmly controlled by unbending conservatives, confronted rising labor unrest in the major industrial centers alongside heightened restlessness among the peripheral national minorities. It was a sign of the times that during the first seven months of 1914 industrial unrest reached unparalleled scope and intensity, much of it politically and socially rather than economically motivated.

Great care must be taken to distinguish between, on the one hand, the actual scope and intensity of these internal tensions and disturbances, and, on the other hand, their perception, evaluation, and exploitation by the political contestants of the time. It is characteristic of prerevolutionary situations that hardened conservatives and counterrevolutionaries deliberately exaggerate all disorders, including the imminence of their transmutation into full-scale insurrection, in order to press and justify energetic precautionary measures. In turn, advanced reformers and revolutionaries similarly distort and distrust the intentions and actions of their domestic antagonists, charging them with preemptive counterrevolutionary design. But this mutual misrepresentation itself contributed to the polarization between the intransigent forces of order and the revolutionary forces of change, at the expense of the moderate, compromise-seeking center.

In Britain, France, and Italy parliamentary liberalism — the locus of this vital center — was heavily besieged, if not on the verge of collapse. . . . In Germany, Austria-Hungary, and Russia, where the ruling power elite considered even the advocates of integral parliamentarianism dangerous revolutionaries, the vital center was almost completely emasculated.

It would seem that in these as in other prerevolutionary eras, the specter of revolution precipitated an active counterrevolutionary response among vulnerable status groups — the landed aristocracy, the petty nobility, the petite-bourgeoisie, the artisans, and the by-passed entrepreneurs. In fact, there may well be a certain parallelism between the attitudes and actions of such crisis strata in domestic politics and the attitudes and actions of foreign-policy actors who consider the nation's international power and prestige to be declining. In both instances the threatened parties are particularly prone to force a preemptive showdown — armed repression or insurrection at home or preventive war abroad — with the resolve of thereby arresting or reversing the course of history, which they claim to be turning against them. . . .

Evidently foreign-policy issues became highly politicized, since notwithstanding governmental appeals, the primacy of foreign policy is inoperative under prerevolutionary conditions. Whereas the campaign against the arms race was an integral part of the struggle against the forces of order, the campaign for preparedness was a central feature of the struggle against the forces of change. All along the superpatriots of the two opposing camps did each other's bidding in that they exploited and fomented the mutual suspicion, fear, hostility and insecurity that quickened the European arms race. . . . In brief, the center increasingly relied on the right as a backstop, with the powerful encouragement of the upper echelons of the army, the foreign offices, the diplomatic corps, the ministry of the interior, and — in most cases — the church. Almost without exception these time-honored institutions were strongholds of the threatened and intransigent crisis strata rather than of the self-confident and supple business and banking grande-bourgeoisie.

To a not inconsiderable degree, then, throughout Europe the rising international tensions were accompanied by rising internal tensions — by mounting social, political, and economic struggles that radicalized the extremes, eroded the center, and inclined the governments to push preparedness and diplomatic obduracy as part of their efforts to maintain a precarious domestic status quo.

Wolfgang J. Mommsen

Domestic Factors in German Foreign Policy

Wolfgang Mommsen, professor of modern history at Düsseldorf University, is best known for his writings on British and German imperialism as well as for his investigations into the career and influence of Max Weber. In this selection, Mommsen takes a functional approach: he portrays a government structure that was largely devoid of firm direction as a result of crippling domestic influences upon official foreign-policy planning. Faced with this systemic malaise, Bethmann Hollweg withdrew into a world of secrecy and near-isolation; in the end, he opted for war not out of a lust for world power, but out of domestic weakness and confusion in the face of rapid socioeconomic change.

Bethmann Hollweg was alarmed by the warlike spirit prevailing in important sections of German society, and he spoke out strongly against it. But this was of little avail. Although there was no unanimity as to which objectives German policy should go after, the conservative and bourgeois classes tended to agree on one point: that Germany should act more vigorously whenever a new opportunity arose to acquire new territories abroad, perhaps even at the risk of a major war. Thus as early as 1912 there developed a political constellation which foreshadowed the situation that existed in the first years of the war. On the one side we find a government which, although in favor of an expansionist policy, attempted to pursue an essentially moderate course. On the other side there were strong groups within the upper classes, supported by important sections of the parties, which advocated a vigorous foreign policy, and which entertained the notion that if Germany could not get her way otherwise she should not shrink from taking up arms. . . .

From Wolfgang J. Mommsen, "Domestic Factors in German Foreign Policy Before 1914," *Central European History*, v. 6 (March 1973), pp. 24–43. Reprinted by permission of the author.

This can be explained only by taking into account the peculiar nature of the political system of Wilhelmine Germany in the prewar years. Since the turn of the century the internal situation had undergone substantial changes, and it may be said that the governmental system was no longer in line with the social structures emerging in the course of an accelerating process of industrialization. The social basis of traditional conservatism was dwindling away. It was not only the shift from a primarily agricultural society toward urban industrialism which made life more and more difficult for the Conservatives. It was rather the increasing speed of social mobilization, associated with a growing diversification of incomes, which cut into those sections of the population which up to then had been oriented to traditionalist values and life-expectations. From the socioeconomic point of view, the upper middle class was about to become the dominant group in German society. It was only the rapid growth of the working-class movement which afforded the conservatives another lease on political predominance. . . . Measured in socioeconomic terms, the agrarian and, in particular, the petit-bourgeois sections of German society were still in the majority. . . . It is these social groups which were all too ready to lend their support to traditionalist and conservative politics, and upon whose sympathy the pseudoconstitutional governments of Bülow and Bethmann Hollweg could still count.

The traditionalist sections of German society were still remarkably strong, yet were no longer a sufficient basis for an outright conservative policy. Neither did the opposite possibility exist. The parties which could be called "progressive," namely the Social Democrats, the Progressives, a part of the National Liberals, and to some degree the left wing of the Center Party, were on the ascendant, but for the time being did not possess a majority. In spite of their great success in the Reichstag elections of 1912, the Social Democrats and Progressives were unable to exert any substantial influence on actual legislation. . . . Whenever the bourgeois parties were about to join forces with the Social Democrats on a particular issue, the government almost always succeeded in bringing them to heel again by pointing out that such behavior was contrary to the national interest. . . . Both the Social Democrats and the National Liberals were tied down by traditional attitudes which made any compromise extremely difficult. This situation was intensified by the socioeconomic situation: after 1909 class conflicts had again become more tense. . . .

The almost complete deadlock in parliamentary politics which was caused in part by the antagonism between the Social Democrats and the liberal parties originated, in the last analysis, in the deep antagonisms within German society, which had been intensified by the momentous economic growth. None of the major political groups . . . were at that time in a position to alter things substantially. The Conservatives, supported by the right wing of the Prussian National Liberals, controlled a strong defensive position thanks to their enormous strength in both houses of the Prussian *Landtag*. The Center Party and the National Liberals, although less and less inclined to join the conservative camp, were not strong enough to pursue a policy of moderate reform and at the same time to check effectively the further growth of the Social Democrats. The latter party was given almost no chance to exercise an effective influence on the course of politics, and the Social Democrats were rightly worried by symptoms which indicated that the potential reservoir of voters was approaching the point of exhaustion.

It was only this situation which enabled the semi-authoritarian government of Bethmann Hollweg to carry on in spite of its unpopularity in all political quarters. To put it another way, the stalemate of the party system was the main source of Bethmann Hollweg's relative strength. . . . Bethmann Hollweg thought it best to keep clear of the parties as much as possible, and if possible to restrict the influence of the party leaders on the actual decision-making. However, maintaining a policy "above the parties" was bound to multiply the inherent evils of all authoritarian rule. Official policy and party politics were pursued side by side, with insufficient communication between them. This was the case in particular with foreign policy. Traditionally the Reichstag had no say at all in these matters, and so the chancellor did not care to inform the party leaders properly about the actual difficulties of German foreign policy; superficial consultations, followed up by appeals for support on national grounds, were still considered sufficient. Under these conditions the party leaders could afford to give themselves up to a rather irresponsible nationalist agitation, all the more so because they had to compete with extraparliamentary associations like the Pan-German League and the *Wehrverein*. As there was no proper exchange of political opinions between the government and the country at large, the gap between the ideologies of the day and the realities became wider and wider. . . .

Both the high bureaucracy and the officer corps, however, became more and more worried about the increasingly rapid advance of democratic ideas within German society. The officer corps was particularly sensitive to this trend; it therefore reacted disproportionately against any encroachment on its traditional rights by the Reichstag or public opinion. Bethmann Hollweg had a very difficult time clearing himself of the charges made against him in military quarters and court circles that he had not defended the rights of the army energetically enough during the debates in the Finance Committee of the Reichstag on the armament bill of 1913. William II considered the *Kommandogewalt* [supreme command authority] the last vestige of supreme monarchical power. . . .

William II and the military establishment considered it the most important task of any chancellor to keep the Reichstag in check. Yet it became more and more evident that this was an impossible task, even under such favorable conditions as those of Wilhelmine Germany. The general trend toward more popular, if not democratic, forms of government made itself felt in German society as well as elsewhere, and resulted among other things in an enhanced self-consciousness of the Reichstag. It was no longer possible to discard the political requests of the Reichstag altogether. Conversely, the Conservatives and their fellow travellers were panic-stricken, and at least some of them felt that they were standing with their backs to the wall. In such a situation it was difficult to work out compromises, both on the social level and on the political level. . . . Bethmann Hollweg dared not seek political support on the Left . . . [and] he refused to join forces with the Right. . . . Bethmann Hollweg's "policy of the diagonal," which did not please anybody, was a genuinely conservative policy.

The dissent within the ruling elite as to whether this kind of policy was right made itself felt, of course, in the sphere of foreign policy just as much as in internal affairs. In a way, Bethmann Hollweg deliberately discounted public opinion in matters of foreign policy, but he could afford to do so only if all sections of the government were willing to take a common stand on controversial issues vis-à-vis public opinion. The chancellor, however, became less and less capable of seeing that this principle was adhered to.

The chancellor believed that the only way out was to conduct foreign policy in almost absolute secrecy, holding back from the public at large, and even from the party leaders, all but the most elementary information. Bethmann Hollweg was fully aware that by doing this he exposed himself to vicious attacks from Conservatives and extreme nationalists alike, as his policy inevitably appeared to outsiders inconsistent and weak. In spite of this unfortunate fact, he refused to put forward any specific program. He did not act upon suggestions by Rathenau to give the country a lead in matters of foreign policy, being convinced that publicity was bound to impair the chances of ultimate success. Riezler wrote at the time, not without some conceit, that only a foreign policy which did *not* care for the applause of the public, and which was *not* heading for quick results, was likely to achieve anything worthwhile.

There can be no doubt that the government of Bethmann Hollweg did not seriously contemplate attaining any of its objectives by war until May–June 1914 — with the possible exception of a liquidation of the Ottoman Empire taking place without the Germans getting a proper share. Bethmann Hollweg was confident that he could get along without a war, although by the end of 1913 he became increasingly worried about the deteriorating position of the German Empire within the European system of powers. He stuck to a peaceful policy, all the more because he was convinced that the existing political order probably would not survive a war. Fritz Fischer has argued again and again that Bethmann Hollweg's repeated attempts to negotiate a neutrality agreement with Great Britain were part and parcel of a policy of expansion by means of war. Britain should be made to stand aside in order to allow Germany safely to crush France and Russia — this, he maintains, was the core of German calculations. This is, however, not borne out by the sources. It will have to be admitted that a neutrality agreement . . . played, so to speak, a token role in the internal struggle between Tirpitz and William II on one side, and Bethmann Hollweg and the Foreign Office on the other. This state of affairs existed behind the scenes during and after the visit of Lord Haldane to Berlin in February 1912. . . .

It is at this point that pressure from the public at large also has to be given proper attention. The relations among the military establishment, the court, and the Conservatives were, of course, fairly intimate. In conservative quarters, as well as in the Pan-German League, the assumption was indeed widely held that a war was likely to have a healthy effect on German national character. Furthermore, a war appeared to be convenient in order to set the clock in the interior "right" again. . . .

By far the most serious challenge to Bethmann Hollweg's foreign policy came, however, from the General Staff. The military leaders were extremely concerned about the prospect that the main premise of the Schlieffen Plan, namely, a slow Russian mobilization which would allow the German Army to crush France before the Russians became an effective military danger, was being undermined by the progress of Russian armaments, and in particular by the completion of the railways in western Russia. Their apprehensions were not reduced by the rather ambiguous official Russian reaction to press charges that Russia was preparing a war against Germany. In May or June 1914 Moltke therefore suggested that the government ought to bring about a war, while Germany was still in a position to win it. Obviously, the idea of a preventive war was gaining ground in governmental quarters. Even William II, who despite all his militaristic pathos was essentially in favor of peace, was in doubt as to whether it might not be wiser to take up arms before the Russian armament program was completed, as he confided to [Max] Warburg in June 1914.

Outside the inner circle of the government other considerations also came into play. Quite a few people, such as Heydebrandt [*sic*] und der Lasa, maintained that a war would be a splendid opportunity to smash the Social Democrats. Bethmann Hollweg was furious about such "nonsense," presumably because he was aware of the consequences for his political position if such views were taken up by the emperor. Bethmann Hollweg emphatically denied that a European war would strengthen the case of the conservatives. Rather, it was likely to benefit the Social Democrats; it might even result in the dethronement of some monarchs. The somewhat scanty sources do not allow all too radical conclusions; yet it can be gathered from them that Bethmann Hollweg and Jagow apparently had a difficult time fending off such ideas. They were careful to make clear that they were not, in principle, against the idea of a preventive war — any other stand might have been interpreted as weakness — yet they nonetheless took exception to the suggestion of solving the problems of German diplomacy by a preventive war. Their main argument was that in view of the improving relations with Great Britain it would be folly to pursue such a policy. . . .

The political calculation of the German government amounted to gambling with very high stakes indeed. Bethmann Hollweg himself called it "a leap in the dark" which was dictated by the "most severe duty." The chancellor's position was no longer strong enough to get any alternative accepted by the inner ring of the ruling elite. His plan was a fairly precise reflection of the deep division within the government itself. It was a compromise between two rival schemes. It did not directly work for war; rather, it favored a diplomatic solution of the crisis. Still, it satisfied the request of the military establishment insofar as it did nothing to avoid war. The attempt to maneuver Russia into a position in which *she* would have to decide about peace or war was not dictated only by the consideration that otherwise the Social Democrats might not rally behind the government. It was equally influenced by the calculation that only in this way could the forthcoming crisis be exploited diplomatically, and with the afterthought that, provided the Russians shrank back from extreme measures, the fears of the German General Staff could be positively disproved.

Hence, it was not so much lust for world power as weakness and confusion which induced Bethmann Hollweg to embark on such a political strategy. The contradictions which can be discovered in the calculations of the German government in July 1914 are a rather precise reflection of the sharp antagonisms within the German ruling elite. It must be added, however, that this was possible only because those groups which were part of the elite (namely, the upper stratum of the governmental bureaucracy, the General Staff and behind it the officer corps, and the conservative entourage of the emperor) enjoyed a political influence which was out of proportion to their actual importance in German society as a whole. This was partly due to the fact that the stalemate on the level of parliamentary politics had enabled the government to carry on with its policies as if nothing had happened at all. It is noteworthy that the government could afford to disregard entirely the opinions of the party leaders in July 1914. . . .

In the last analysis, we may conclude, the causes of the First World War must be sought not in the blunders and miscalculations of the governments alone, but in the fact that Germany's governmental system, as well as Austria-Hungary's and Russia's, was no longer adequate in the face of rapid social change and the steady advance of mass politics.

The Mood of 1914: German soldiers on their way to Paris. (The Bettmann Archive)

The Outbreak of War: July 1914

Joachim Remak

1914 — Serbia Opts for War

Joachim Remak, professor emeritus at the University of California at Santa Barbara, is best known for *The Gentle Critic: Theodor Fontane and German Politics* and for his edition of documents, *The Nazi Years*. In this selection, from Remak's earlier studies, *Sarajevo* and *The First World War: Causes, Conduct, Consequences*, he reminds us that the July Crisis began in Sarajevo on 28 June 1914 and that Belgrade made the initial decision to risk a general European war to achieve its Great South Slav State aspirations. "The pursuit of Serbia's aims was worth a war with Austria." And with Russia's backing, chances seemed good that those aspirations could be realized.

From Joachim Remak, "1914 — The Third Balkan War: Origins Reconsidered," *Journal of Modern History*, v. 43 (1971) pp. 353–366. Reprinted with permission of The University of Chicago and the author. Footnotes omitted.

But how had the Germans become involved in the first place? Through a minor and obscure Balkan quarrel? Yes, if by obscure we mean that it was insufficiently understood by outsiders, and by minor that no vital interests of the great powers were involved. To the two nations directly affected, however, to Austria and Serbia, few crises could have mattered more, or been clearer in their implications, than Sarajevo. And both nations behaved with great recklessness in 1914.

We have stooped over for too long now, searching for the underlying causes of the war. We have become so involved in subtleties that the obvious has sometimes escaped us; we have not seen the forest for the roots. The obvious fact is that the issue that led to Verdun and Versailles not only was Austro-Serb in origin, but that in the immediate crisis that followed, some of the most basic decisions affecting peace or war were made by Berchtold rather than Bethmann, and by Pašić rather than Sazonov.

It is a moot question which nation practiced the worse sort of brinkmanship. Let us evade it by dealing with them in alphabetical order. As for Austria, then, it was the whole general direction of the Ballplatz's policy after Sarajevo, and the ultimatum of July 23 in particular, that invited war with Serbia, and the wider war as well. What an appalling document it was — tardy, incompetent, deceptive, designed to be rejected. Austria was setting the course, and neither friend nor foe had been allowed an honest look at its direction.

It is entirely possible, of course, to present a case for the defense. Sarajevo was no pretense; the Habsburg monarchy had some perfectly legitimate interests to defend — Serbia was a good deal closer to Austria than southeast Asia is to the United States. Surely, self-preservation is as sensible and honorable a motive as any, and the state one wished to maintain had a great deal to be said in its favor. "All my libido is given to Austria-Hungary," wrote Dr. Freud the day after Serbia's reply had been received. Austria's decision meant "liberation through a bold deed."

What alternative did the Habsburg monarchy have? Its vital interests were involved, in a way those of no other European state were in 1914; not Russia's and not Germany's, not those of France nor of Great Britain. Of all of Europe's crises and conflicts, the Austro-Serbian issue was unique in that it seemed to allow no leeway between either surrender or war. None of the others had "led to actions that produced war. They were either negotiable or repressible. The one problem that was neither negotiable nor repressible was that raised by threats to the integrity of Austria-Hungary."

Still, to understand all is *not* to forgive all. It is true enough that, as a committee of distinguished French and German historians put it in 1952, "the documents do not permit attributing, to any government or nation, a premeditated desire for European war in 1914." But Berchtold and Conrad had very much of a premeditated desire for a simple Balkan war to recover some of the monarchy's lost prestige. Did they want that war to spread? No, but the truth was that the reckless and inadequate people who were deciding policy in Vienna did not really care. This was Austria's war; perhaps only the fact that the countrymen of Johann Strauss and Sigmund Freud ordinarily made such poor villains (there would be some fairly obvious exceptions such as Adolf Hitler) allowed that simple fact to be forgotten so thoroughly.

Austria's war, and Serbia's. Two Austrian victims, seven Bosnian assassins, and no one can say to this day how many Serbian helpers. Sarajevo was more than an excuse for war. It was one of its major causes.

The assassins, in a sense, were innocents. Had he known that his deed might mean war, one of them said during his trial, he would have preferred his own death to that of his victims. But he was speaking for himself, not for Colonel Dimitrijević. Apis was a man who considered the consequences of his actions.

But to what extent did the involvement of Serbia's chief of military intelligence reflect on his government? The assassination, after all, had been planned by the Black Hand during the colonel's off-duty hours, and not by Pašić or any of his ministers. In fact, was not the crime largely a local affair, and is not the question whether any of the assassins even belonged to the Black Hand still unresolved?

Yes and no. Of course the act had its local roots. It involved Young Bosnia as much as Union or Death. Social ferment played its part along with national enthusiasm. The two great trends of nineteenth-century Europe — nationalism and the desire for reforms affecting the land — had not halted at the borders of Bosnia-Herzegovina. "I am from the village," said Princip at his trial. "Nine-tenths of our people are farmers who suffer," said Čabrinović, "who live in misery, who have no schools, who are deprived of any culture. We sympathized with them in their distress . . . we loved our people."

Yes and no. We have complicated things too much. The roots were in Sarajevo, and they were in Belgrade. Each side was using the other. Each could do so without guilt feelings, for each loved their common nation.

Of the seven assassins, two survive to this day. One is the director of a historical institute in Belgrade, the other the curator of the ethnographic department of the Sarajevo museum. In the late sixties this author talked to both, and two questions and answers above all others remain in his mind. Who, if any, were the Black Hand members in the group? Come now, was the answer. Perhaps some, perhaps none. What did it matter? "We have many Black Hands in this part of the world." And the question of motive? He had read all the theories, and they were all of them right, and all of them wrong. "Look, we were seventeen."

We have complicated things too much. Jut what, scholars have asked for years now, did Pašić know about the preparations for Sarajevo; to what extent was the Serbian government involved? Can we trust a disgruntled minister's recollections; can we put any credence in some fragmentary document intercepted by an Austrian border guard? The details are complex; the experts have never been able to agree on them entirely. Yet certain basic truths really are not very complex at all. And among them is the fact that Dimitrijević's action did incriminate the Serbian government, for reasons both long range and immediate. That government had for too many years been tolerating or even encouraging a movement for a Greater Serbia whose aims were bound to be offensive to Austria-Hungary and whose methods were bound to be offensive to anyone. Very specifically speaking, the government in 1914 had taken no effective action to prevent the assassination of Franz Ferdinand, of which it very probably had some foreknowledge, nor had it managed to end the influence of the Black Hand, of which it assuredly had knowledge.

Not that there was anything in the least ignoble about either Pašić's or Dimitrijević's aims. The concept of a Greater South Slav State was fully as defensible as was Austria-Hungary's right to survival. Tragedy, in the Hegelian definition, consists not of the conflict of right with wrong but of right with right. But the Serbians set about achieving their purposes with a truly frightening disregard of the consequences. Here, then, was Serbia's vast share in the responsibility for the First World War, one that was matched only by Austria's;

Belgrade surely knew that it was set on a collision course, yet it would not alter direction. There is, in the British files, a report from the ambassador to Vienna, Sir Fairfax Cartwright, written in January 1913 in the wake of the First Balkan War, which sums up the entire matter better than any later historian can:

> *Servia will some day set Europe by the ears, and bring about a universal war on the Continent. . . . I cannot tell you how exasperated people are getting here at the continual worry which that little country causes to Austria under encouragement from Russia. It may be compared to a certain extent to the trouble we had to suffer through the hostile attitude formerly assumed against us by the Transvaal Republic under the guiding hand of Germany. It will be lucky if Europe succeeds in avoiding war as a result of the present crisis. The next time a Servian crisis arises . . . , I feel sure that Austria-Hungary will refuse to admit of any Russian interference in the dispute and that she will proceed to settle her differences with her little neighbor by herself "coûte que coûte."*

Had Belgrade not been bidding for a Greater Serbia, there could have been a way out even after the Austrian ultimatum. Pǎsić, in that case, could have upset all of Austria's plans by accepting the ultimatum in toto. "Such an acceptance would have made it impossible for the Austrians, in the eyes of world opinion, to start a war, and the few Austrian officials dispatched to Serbia to investigate the assassination would have provided a perfect spectacle of helplessness. The claim that such a mission could not be reconciled with the Serbian constitution cannot be taken very seriously. Worse things had happened in Serbia that were not in accord with the constitution."

No, the reason some Serbians were willing to play the game the way the Austrians wished them to was that they thought the prize justified the stakes, and that with Russia's aid chances were good that the prize might be won. Nor did they play the game at all badly. Their reply to the ultimatum was a triumph — but it was a triumph in public relations rather than in settling the crisis. Which was what Belgrade had in mind. The pursuit of Serbia's aims was worth a war with Austria. And if that war should activate Europe's alliances and bring about an Austro-German-Serbian-Russian-French war, so be it. No fear of international complications, after all, had been capable of forestalling two earlier Balkan wars. Turkey was dying and now Austria was; 1914–18 was the longest but by no means the only war of the Turkish succession. It was the Third Balkan War.

Overlooking Belgrade stands the great Yugoslav World War I memorial, the tomb of the unknown soldier. A vast flight of steps leads up to a sort of temple where eight female figures in black marble represent the nations of Yugoslavia: Serbia, Croatia, Dalmatia, Bosnia, and the rest. On the floor, there is a single inscription, which reads:

1912–1918

Seen that way, Serbia was wholly right in the decision of July 25, and the question of "war guilt" becomes unreal and irrelevant. Of course, so was everybody, right, and one wishes that Versailles had never introduced the concept of guilt. Serbia was right in wanting to expand, Austria in wanting to survive. Germany was right in fearing isolation, Great Britain in fearing German power. Everyone was right. And everyone was wrong, for no one foresaw what war would mean, either in terms of costs or of consequences. All were sinners, all were sinned against.

But then, discussions of causes, like so many other things in history, are constructions after the event. How many people, in 1914, were really that aware of all the origins of the conflict, immediate and long range, that we abstract in leisure from the documents later? How many had thought through every move of the diplomatic game, from Princip's opening to checkmate? Not even Berchtold or Pašić. What most of them did feel — and act on — was that here was another crisis, one that contained great risks, obviously, but that might reasonably be expected to end as noncataclysmically as the diplomatic crises of the past decades had. That it did not, that this time the rhetoric of war would be followed by the reality, none of them foresaw, let alone planned. Only prophets after the event would be able to see the inevitability of arriving, step by step, stage by stage, by a series of moves and countermoves that all seemed logical, reasonable, and containable at the time, at a road which had no turns left. And perhaps, all one can truly say in the end is that World War I was a modern diplomatic crisis gone wrong, the one gamble, or rather series of gambles, that did not work out, the one deterrent that did not deter. It happens.

Samuel R. Williamson, Jr.

Austria-Hungary Opts for War

Samuel Williamson, professor at the University of the South, is best known for his work on Anglo-French grand strategy before 1914; in 1991 he completed *Austria-Hungary and the Origins of the First World War*. In this selection, he argues that Austria-Hungary was more than a mere marionette but Germany less than the driving force behind war. He also suggests that Conrad von Hötzendorf's military planning constituted "a calculated risk to open war."

The events at Sarajevo convinced Berchtold, Stürgkh, and Bilinski, almost without discussion, that this time Belgrade had gone too far. The senior military commanders — Conrad von Hötzendorf, War Minister Krobatin, and the culpable Potiorek in Sarajevo — were, of course, eager to settle accounts with Belgrade. Even the old kaiser turned bellicose and inclined to action. István [Stephan] Tisza raised immediate doubts about a belligerent response, reservations prompted in part by concern that a possible victory might bring territorial acquisitions that would affect Magyar power. By July 3 the senior policymakers, Tisza excepted, were ready for a military confrontation. The psychological step from the tough, abrupt diplomacy of 1913 to war in 1914 was a small one, too easily made and with few second thoughts. All other options had been tried and found wanting.

This belligerency was reinforced, moreover, by Potiorek's alarming (and possibly distorted) reports of widespread disorder in Bosnia-Herzegovina. . . . Potiorek argued that only military measures, including martial law in the two provinces, could restore the situa-

From *Essays on World War I: Origins and Prisoners of War*, pp. 9–36, ed. Samuel R. Williamson, Jr. and Peter Pastor. Copyright 1983 by Social Science Monographs, Columbia University Press.

tion. Quite rightly, no policymaker doubted that the assassins had connections with Belgrade. . . . Faced with what later generations called "wars of national liberation," Franz Joseph's government resolved to protect its one imperial acquisition of the late nineteenth century. Serbia would be punished and Russia, it was hoped, would be prudent enough to stand aside.

Once Berchtold, the key swing man, resolved to fight Serbia, he and Conrad von Hötzendorf faced a set of interlocking problems of implementation: discovering how Berlin would react, convincing Tisza, assessing Russia's intentions, dispatching the ultimatum, and initiating the offensive action.

The first and most celebrated problem was the approach to Berlin. An essential first step in keeping the war with Serbia localized was to deter Russian intervention. Berchtold and Conrad von Hötzendorf believed that unequivocal German support would act as a deterrent to Russian intervention. But this had to be unambiguous support, not the mercurial ups and downs of 1912 and 1913 when Berlin had tilted first in one direction, then in another. Experience also suggested that gaining Germany's consent to the idea of action was easier than winning approval for its tactical implementation. This time Vienna would seek assurances early rather than late.

The man selected to win German support was Berchtold's belligerent, impulsive *chef de cabinet*, Count Hoyos. On July 3 he traveled to Berlin with an amended version of the June memorandum, a letter from Franz Joseph to the German kaiser, and with oral instructions, all of which left no doubt that Vienna would attack Serbia. Berlin, as Fritz Fischer and others have exhaustively shown, had its own reasons for readily giving the Habsburgs a "blank check." But it was Vienna that first resolved for war, that sought German assurances, and that exploited them once received. In the critical early days of July the initiative rested with the Danubian leadership, not vice versa. Sidney Fay's earlier assessment retains much validity: "The Kaiser and his advisors on July 5 and 6 were not criminals plotting the World War; they were simpletons putting 'a noose about their necks' and handing the other end of the rope to a stupid and clumsy adventurer who now felt free to go as far as he liked." What happened was a fateful meshing of aggressive German *Weltpolitik* with an even more aggressive, irresponsible Habsburg *Balkanpolitik.* . . .

In any case, once Berchtold had his "blank check," he became progressively less cooperative with Berlin. Ambassador Heinrich von Tschirschky had easy access to Berchtold in early July, indeed even participated in Count Hoyos's briefing of the foreign minister and other ministers on July 7. Thereafter he followed the efforts to convince Tisza to endorse an openly belligerent course and duly reported Vienna's apparently dilatory posture. While subsequently not directly involved, he reported on the pace of Habsburg action, the framing of the ultimatum, and the stage-managing of Habsburg tactics before July 23, such as Conrad von Hötzendorf's decision to go on vacation. After July 7 the Habsburg apparatus released minimal information to its German ally. Possibly Berchtold appreciated, from past experience, that too high a profile might prompt a change of heart in Berlin. This time he took no chances. Thus throughout July he set the pace (however much the Germans disliked its tempo), defined the moves, and closed off the options.

The Hoyos mission had another crucial ramification as well. It furnished Berchtold with added leverage in dealing with István Tisza's reluctance for a military solution. An advocate of caution, the Magyar leader preferred a slower pace. Instead Berchtold outmaneuvered him, first by dispatching Hoyos to Berlin, and then by getting a surprisingly strong answer of apparently limitless German support. Outflanked, the minister president found himself the only holdout in the Common Cabinet against Berchtold's desire to plunge ahead. In the cabinet meeting on July 7 Tisza argued against the idea of a local war, but convinced no one else. And by the end of the session even his opposition had weakened. Yet Tisza continued to argue the diplomatic case, sending a new memorandum to Franz Joseph on July 8 in which he advocated hesitation and prudence. But the old kaiser, now also ready for quick, decisive action, remained unmoved. Berchtold and others continued to remind Tisza of their German support. Under this pressure Tisza slowly altered his position. On July 14, when he went back to Vienna, he finally approved a military course. . . . Hoyos's trip to Berlin and Tisza's subsequent isolation helped to eliminate the most important constitutional barrier to military action against Serbia.

Tisza's obstinacy gained one apparent concession for Budapest. Berchtold, then later the Common Cabinet on July 19 when it met to approve the ultimatum, agreed that the monarchy would seek no

substantial territorial gains from a defeated Serbia. . . . Yet this concession had a hollow ring, best illustrated by Conrad von Hötzendorf's alleged comment when the July 19 meeting broke up: "Well,
we shall see. Before the Balkan War, the powers talked about the *status quo*. After the war, nobody bothered about it any more." And in
August, well before Bethmann-Hollweg's famous September memorandum, planners in the Ballhausplatz were developing territorial
ambitions toward Poland that clearly betokened what Tisza feared
most: some form of trialism involving the Slavs instead of
German-Magyar dualism. At most Tisza won only a Pyrrhic victory
in his struggle with Berchtold during the July crisis.

Berchtold's third problem was Russia: what would it do? It was
not a new problem: it had had to be considered in 1912 and 1913. At
that time two contradictory analyses had emerged. The pessimistic
one held that Russia, in contrast to its pacific behavior of 1909,
would not again stand aside; an attack on Belgrade would launch a
European war. Even Conrad von Hötzendorf occasionally subscribed
to this estimate. The optimistic assessment argued that Russia was
not yet ready to intervene, its military recovery from its Japanese
defeat not yet complete. To this some added that Russia would not
intervene because war would once more pose the threat of revolution. For these reasons some policymakers believed St. Petersburg
would fulminate — but no more — if Vienna moved against Belgrade. And they contended that, if Berlin stood resolutely behind the
monarchy, the Russians would be deterred altogether. Throughout
the successive war-peace crises of 1912 and 1913, these visions of
Russia's probable behavior had vied with each other, usually in
approximate cautionary balance.

Possibly the most striking feature of the Habsburg
decision-making process in July 1914 was its failure to think seriously
anew about Russia's position and its possible intervention. The policymakers acted as if Russia did not exist. Possibly they were overcon-
fident about the deterrent effect of Berlin's "blank check"; possibly
they exaggerated Romanov adherence to the principle of monarchical solidarity and the need to avenge the Sarajevo murders. Certainly
they failed to pay even elementary attention to the danger signals of
Russian military response. Until late in the whole process, the senior
leadership blissfully directed its attention only southward. In almost
classic, cybernetic fashion, Berchtold, Conrad von Hötzendorf and

the others, now programmed for action against Serbia, disregarded any information that might require them to modify their plans — and ambitions. They would do what they wanted and, of course, preferred to do: fight Serbia.

Berchtold's fourth problem centered around the dispatch of an unacceptable ultimatum to Belgrade. Commentators have frequently asserted that, had Vienna moved more quickly in July 1914, it might have exploited a reservoir of European sympathy and been allowed to punish Belgrade. Moreover, swift action would have eliminated the later accusation that Vienna lulled Europe into somnolence, only to precipitate a crisis. These assessments merit two observations. First, the Habsburg armies were incapable of a quick, decisive strike against Serbia, or even the speedy seizure of, say, Belgrade. Conrad von Hötzendorf's insistence on a total attack had eliminated such possibilities, leaving Plan B (fourteen to sixteen days for mobilization) as the only alternative. A swift surprise move was neither programmatically nor temperamentally an option for Vienna.

Second, a fundamental organizational arrangement virtually ruled out immediate action that would contain any element of surprise. On July 6 half the military strength of Agram (Zagreb), Innsbruck, Kaschau (Kosice), Temesvar (Timisoara), Budapest, Pressburg (Bratislava) and Graz was away on "harvest leave." If these troops were recalled to their units, their return would immediately be detected. This in turn would deprive the Habsburg decisionmakers of any chance for even modest surprise, alarm the other powers, probably disrupt the mobilization process, and — not without grave consequences — leave the crops unharvested. Instead of recalling these troops, it was better, from Conrad von Hötzendorf's viewpoint, quietly to cancel all remaining leaves and let the others expire on schedule between July 19 and July 25. It is this consideration that helps explain Conrad von Hötzendorf's relative lack of concern over the timing of military action against Serbia, that accounts for Berchtold's leisurely pace in his treatment of Tisza, and that explains the ultimatum's clash with the French state visit to St. Petersburg. An innocuous organizational measure, taken years earlier by Conrad von Hötzendorf to help to bring in the harvest, paradoxically handicapped the Austro-Hungarian generals and diplomats alike in the moment of supreme crisis.

The final problem in launching a local war was Conrad von Hötzendorf's own: which offensive scheme to implement — Plan B [Serbia] or Plan R [Russia]? In actuality, he drew from both and failed with each. . . . By going south, Conrad von Hötzendorf would have the war he wanted, earlier and less ambiguously. Had he opted for Plan R, he would have been on the defensive in the south, with no guarantee of an Austro-Hungarian offensive attack on Serbia. If he adopted Plan R and planned for the offensive in the north, the actual fighting would not begin for almost three weeks, a week longer than Plan B. This additional week, he may have concluded, would allow more time for diplomatic intrusions and the possibility of peace. By launching the attack on Serbia, even if it was later to be reduced, he was at war more quickly. And Conrad von Hötzendorf knew that any war, once under way, is not easily stopped by political intervention. . . . By moving south Conrad von Hötzendorf, whatever his later comments, ensured the military denouement that he so passionately believed was essential to the survival of the Habsburg state. The strategic blunder was part of a calculated risk to open war — and it worked.

In 1914 Austria-Hungary was not an innocent, middle-level government pressured into war by its more aggressive, ambitious northern ally. Rather those in power in Vienna were determined to control and fulfill the only international mission left to the Habsburgs: benevolent supervision of the Balkans. To do so, effectively and without interruption, required, so they believed, the reduction or elimination of the most potent internal danger to the monarchy — the South Slav problem. Serbia's continued appeals to the South Slavs, even a Serbia backed by Russia, could no longer be tolerated if the monarchy were to survive. After the Balkan Wars began in October 1912, Berchtold worked desperately, and with some success, to protect Habsburg interests. He blocked Serbia's access to the Adriatic and created Albania as a potential counterbalance. At each step the foreign minister faced the temptation to abandon diplomacy in favor of force. He rejected it, yet gradually he grew convinced that Serbia understood only threats. Lesser options appeared inappropriate, even self-defeating. Prestige, monarchical self-esteem, exhaustion of patience and imagination — all lured Vienna into a military campaign. Military values, mixed with illusions about Russia and the nature of modern war, acquired an unassailable position. Even Tisza, once he became convinced of the need for military action, became its most ardent proponent. In 1914 the Habsburg decisionmakers, like their German counterparts, were in a *Kriegslust* frame of mind. All that was needed was a pretext.

If viewed from this perspective, the interaction between Berlin and Vienna assumes a different balance and proportion. Certainly it is incorrect to focus all attention on Berlin, or to suggest that Vienna was merely a marionette in the July crisis. It must be remembered that Berchtold eventually joined Conrad von Hötzendorf and the military in pressing for military action. Ironically the most assertive phase of Berchtold's diplomacy was also its most dangerous. In July 1914 peace gave way to war; desperation, hope, blind faith, illusion, exhaustion, and a mix of military ambition overcame the prudence and caution of the earlier Balkan crises. The monarchy at length opted for a draconian solution; the results were equally draconian and devastating. War brought not victory and a solution to the South Slav problem, but defeat and dissolution. From that result momentous consequences still flow.

Fritz Fischer

1914: Germany Opts for War, "Now or Never"

Fritz Fischer, professor emeritus at Hamburg University, rocked the history profession in 1961 with his first book, *Griff nach der Weltmacht*, in which he argued that Germany, inspired by economic interests, sought to achieve world power. More, Fischer suggested that there was continuity in German aims from 1900 to the Second World War. In his second book, from which this selection is taken, based in large measure on the two-volume documentary record published by his student Imanuel Geiss, Fischer presented his argument in even sharper tones, insisting that Germany took Austria-Hungary "on the leash" in its aggressive, expansionist war policy during the July crisis of 1914.

The Occasion Is Propitious — The First Week in July

On 26 June, the German publicist Viktor Naumann traveled to Vienna. He had paid a call at the Foreign Office immediately before his departure and had been informed in detail by Wilhelm von Stumm about the general political situation, the crisis in the Balkans, and the indecisive foreign policy of Austria-Hungary.

When, after the assassination of the Archduke on Sunday, 28 June, at Sarajevo, Naumann repeatedly advised the Austrian foreign minister [Berchtold] and other leading officials at the Ballhausplatz to use the opportunity to "settle accounts" with Serbia, he undoubtedly knew that the same general views of the situation were held by the German Foreign Office. In conversations with Berchtold and Hoyos, Naumann sought to convince Austro-Hungarian politicians that the destruction of Serbia was a matter of life and death for Austria-Hungary. Vienna should present the idea to Berlin in a suitable

From Fritz Fischer, *Krieg der Illusionen. Die deutsche Politik von 1911 bis 1914*, Copyright © 1969 and 1978 by Droste Verlag, Düsseldorf, West Germany. Second Edition 1987. Reprinted by permission of the publisher. Translated by Holger H. Herwig.

form. He was certain that, unlike the year before, in addition to the military, the Foreign Ministry and the emperor no longer objected to a preventive war against Russia, and furthermore, that public opinion would force the government into a war. Also unlike the year before, England's neutrality in a European war was now assured, as was that of Rumania and Greece; one could count upon the cooperation of Bulgaria and Turkey. In the Foreign Office, "one considered the moment propitious in order to bring about the great decision." Naumann warned that if Austria-Hungary did not seize this opportunity, Germany would drop Austria as an ally. Naumann's line of argument corresponded to that of the Foreign Office in the days and weeks ahead.

Like Naumann, German ambassador von Tschirschky also made it clear from the beginning in conversations with Berchtold and in an audience with Emperor Franz Joseph that Germany would support Austria-Hungary if it took forceful action against Serbia, and also promised to protect Austria's rear against Russia — provided that Austria-Hungary formulated a clear and firm plan of action and presented it to Berlin. On 2 July, Tschirschky informed Berchtold: "As the minister knows, Germany repeatedly had announced during the crisis that with regard to Balkan policy, it would always stand behind us (Austria-Hungary)." He pointed out "that in his view only forceful action against Serbia could bring success." That same day, he assured Emperor Franz Joseph that he "could count on finding Germany solidly behind the Monarchy when it came to defense of one of its vital interests." And even if it must be left up to the Monarchy to decide what steps were to be taken, as Tschirschky respectfully put it, he nevertheless could "only repeat that [Emperor Wilhelm] would stand behind every firm decision on the part of Austria-Hungary." This declaration already anticipated the essential points of the promise that Emperor Wilhelm made to the Austrians on 5 July.

On the evening of the same day, 2 July, Franz Joseph signed his personal letter to Wilhelm II, which his special envoy, Count Hoyos, took to Berlin two days later — and in which was stated the intention to eliminate Serbia as a political power factor in the Balkans, to isolate it, and to reduce it in size.

While grave decisions were in reality being considered in Berlin and a feverish activity took place behind the scenes, official Berlin sought to deceive its own populace as well as foreign diplomats by presenting the picture of a city in the midst of summer vacations. Only Under-Secretary of State Zimmermann stayed on at the Foreign Office, and he continuously conducted reassuring talks with foreign diplomats; the State Secretary of the Imperial Navy Office, Tirpitz, and the Chief of the General Staff, Moltke, likewise were on holidays. German officials kept up the comedy even with regard to their Austrian ally. For, when on the morning of 5 July, Ambassador Szögyény handed the chef-de-cabinet Franz Joseph's handwritten letter for Emperor Wilhelm, which had been brought up by Count Hoyos, the Germans pretended to Szögyény that before being able to answer Austria, the emperor would first have to consult Bethmann Hollweg, who was at his estate of Hohenfinow and whom he was recalling to Potsdam for this purpose for the first time since 29 June. But in fact, Bethmann Hollweg had spent every day of the period between 29 June and 5 July — with the exception of 1 and 3 July — at Potsdam and had discussed the political situation with the emperor there.

Various witnesses attest that from the week of the assassination at Sarajevo (Sunday, 28 June) to the Austrian ambassador's audience with Wilhelm II (Sunday, 5 July), government circles in Berlin were of the opinion that the moment was propitious for a European war. On Thursday, 2 July, the Saxon ambassador at Berlin, Salza und Lichtenau, learned at the Foreign Office that the Serbo-Austrian conflict was not thought likely to develop into a Serbo-Austrian war; however, should it prove impossible to avoid such a war, Russia would mobilize "and the world war . . . could no longer be averted." [Salza reported to Dresden,]

> *The military are now urging once again that we should let it come to war, given that Russia is not yet ready.*

However, Salza could not imagine that Wilhelm II would allow himself to be "inveigled" into a war. At the Foreign Office, people were optimistic with regard to the military preparedness of Germany's neighbors:

> *France is too occupied with its domestic affairs and its financial calamity. There may be sabre rattling in Russia, but the only reason for this seems to be that Russia, if at all possible, would like to receive this year already the 500 million that France has promised for next year, because it, too, suffers from a shortage of money.*

England also does not want war because it fears for its trade, has difficulties with its colonies, and respects the German fleet as a "factor with which England now must reckon."

On Friday, 3 July, the Saxon military plenipotentiary at Berlin, Leuckart, had a conversation with the Quartermaster-General of the Great General Staff, Count Waldersee. The latter indicated "that we could be involved in a war from one day to the next. Everything would depend upon the attitude that Russia took toward the Austro-Serbian affair." Leuckart came to the conclusion that the General Staff "thought that it would be quite propitious were a war to come about now. The situation and the prospects would not improve for us." However, according to Leuckart's information, the emperor allegedly "had expressed himself in favor of preserving the peace." Wilhelm II's marginalia of the same day on a report from Tschirschky show that this rumor was false. "Now or never. . . . We must make a clean sweep of the Serbs, and soon," the emperor demanded. Salza's contact at the Foreign Office had linked the prospect of preserving the peace with there being *no* war between Serbia and Austria-Hungary. But two days later, on 4 July, Austria-Hungary was again urged to take precisely this step. On that day, the Viennese correspondent of the *Frankfurter Zeitung*, Ganz, on the instructions of the German ambassador Tschirschky, declared at the Foreign Ministry in Vienna:

> *Germany would support the Monarchy through thick and thin, regardless of what the latter would decide to do against Serbia . . . the sooner Austria-Hungary started, the better. Yesterday would have been better than today, but today is better than tomorrow.*

So as not to leave any doubt about the determination of the German government, Ambassador Tschirschky underlined this promise:

> *Even if the German press, which today is totally anti-Serb, were again to trumpet peace, one should not become confused in Vienna; Emperor and Empire will stand by Austria-Hungary unconditionally. One Great Power could not speak more frankly to another.*

Count Hoyos was thus able to travel to Berlin certain in the knowledge that Franz Joseph's inquiry, which the Austrians had been encouraged to make by Berlin, would receive a favorable reply. This inquiry, put forth in the imperial handwritten letter as well as in a memorandum concerning a new Balkan policy on the part of the

Triple Alliance, did not contain a specific military proposal for a war between Austria-Hungary and Serbia. . . . Rather, the documents contained suggestions for a long-term Balkan policy for the Triple Alliance aimed at reducing Russia's influence in the Balkans by drawing Bulgaria into the Triple Alliance, by making Rumania abandon its growing friendship with Russia and Serbia, by reconciling Greece with Bulgaria and Turkey, and by attracting it also to the Triple Alliance so as to isolate Serbia, the bulwark of anti-Austrian agitation. This regrouping could only be achieved if "Serbia . . . is eliminated as a political power factor in the Balkans." The absence of concrete measures in the memorandum is due to the fact that it had been prepared before the assassination [of the Archduke]. . . . After the assassination, the memorandum was revised once more. Above all, greater weight was now put on the arguments that emphasized the threat not only to Austria-Hungary, but also to Germany. The picture of an incessantly growing, heavily armed Russian colossus and of a France lusting for revenge was now stressed:

> *For, if Russia, assisted by France, tries to unite the Balkan states against Austria-Hungary . . . then this hostility is directed not just against the Monarchy as such, but no less against the ally of the German Empire, against the most vulnerable part of the Central European bloc, which is most exposed due to its geographical situation and internal structure and which blocks the realization of Russia's world political plans.*

This line of argument was designed precisely to appeal to Wilhelm's thought. After all, he was afraid that Germany's world position would be blocked by a pincer movement by the Franco-Russian alliance.

Having for days had his chancellor and the military impress upon him that Austria-Hungary needed to use the situation for a reckoning with Serbia — even at the risk of a European war because *now* was a propitious moment — Wilhelm II interpreted the memorandum to mean that Austria had decided upon military action. He admitted to the Austrian ambassador "that he had expected serious action by us [that is, by Austria] against Serbia," yet he had realized that this action could lead to "a serious European complication," but that even then, "Germany with its customary loyalty would stand at our [that is, Austria's] side." At the same time, he attempted to reassure his ally that Russia was by no means ready for war, and that it would think twice before "appealing to arms." That is why, however much he respected Franz Joseph's well-known love of peace, he would very much regret it, "were we [that is, Austria] to let the moment, which is so propitious for us, pass." The emperor reassured his (Austrian) ally concerning Rumania's attitude: "King Carol and his advisers [will] behave correctly."

On the afternoon of 5 July, Bethmann Hollweg, having studied the memorandum at the Foreign Office that noon, briefed the emperor at Potsdam. He officially seconded the imperial assurance and thereby gave it the constitutional sanction that the Austrian ambassador deemed necessary. . . .

After Austria-Hungary had been committed to military action against Serbia on 5 and 6 July by its official inquiry and the German emperor by his reply to Vienna, the chancellor decided to calm world opinion by sending the military on leave and the emperor on his North Sea cruise. With the emperor's departure from Berlin, Bethmann Hollweg moreover had eliminated one unpredictable factor in German policy. How much the emperor saw himself as such was confirmed by him during a conversation that he had on the evening of 6 July in Kiel with his friend Krupp von Bohlen und Halbach, during which he told him of the impending Austrian action and the German promise. During the course of the conversation, as Krupp noted with embarrassment, [Wilhelm] assured Krupp three times: "This time I shall not cave in." "The repeated imperial assurance that this time no one could again accuse him of irresolution had an almost comic effect." Wilhelm swore that he would respond to a Russian mobilization (which could be expected as a result of the Austrian action against Serbia) with war.

Bethmann Hollweg himself returned to Hohenfinow on the evening of 6 July, in order — linked with Berlin by a telegraph station, which had been specially installed and which was now in operation for over four weeks — to await the Austro-Hungarian action, which, in his view, should happen as quickly as possible.

In evening conversations, as noted by his personal secretary Riezler, his thoughts circled around the recently undertaken weighty decisions. On the one hand, he feared the unreliability of Austrian policy (6 July). . . . But on the other hand, the threatening power of Russia swam before his eyes — the military power of Russia was growing rapidly (6 July) and "the future belongs to Russia, which grows and grows and presses on us as an increasingly more menacing nightmare" (7 July). . . . In spite of his personal scruples, there is no doubt that in the summer of 1914 the imperial chancellor had included a European war in his political calculations, and that he regarded the constellation as especially propitious insofar as this time it was Austria-Hungary and not (as during the Moroccan crisis) the German Empire that was the power primarily affected. . . . Bethmann Hollweg clearly calculated the European war as the first alternative in his policy, and [viewed] a mere diplomatic success only as a second, less desirable, alternative. . . .

"Landgrave, Stand Firm": 8–23 July

While the German government had been determined since early July 1914 to exploit this favorable opportunity in order to wage war against France and Russia, the government at Vienna, while decided on firm steps against Serbia, nevertheless was looking for ways to avoid a military intervention by Russia — although all ministers were convinced that this was unavoidable. At the meeting of the Joint Ministerial Council in Vienna, which took place on 7 July after Count Hoyos's return from Berlin, all ministers spoke in favor of a settling of accounts with Serbia. With the exception of the Hungarian minister president, Tisza, all those present regarded a war against Serbia as the best solution, even at the risk of Russian intervention. . . .

The Chief of the General Staff, Conrad, who was present at various stages of the meeting in order to answer military questions, advocated an immediate war against Serbia and, if necessary, also against Russia. Berchtold, who likewise had expressed himself in favor of a war against Serbia, had doubts because of Rumania's likely behavior and because of probable Italian demands for compensation. Yet, at the same time he was under heavy German pressure. On 8 July, Tschirschky sought him out again to tell him "most emphatically" that "one expects an action against Serbia in Berlin." Berchtold understood from Tschirschky's remarks (as he told Tisza):

> that in Germany any accommodation by us with Serbia would be interpreted as a confession of weakness, which could not but have repercussions on our position within the Triple Alliance and on Germany's future policy.

The Austrian prime minister, Stürgkh, had expressed a similar fear a day before at the Joint Ministerial Council:

> [Austria ran] the risk that by a policy of hesitation and weakness . . . it would later on no longer be so certain of Germany's unqualified support.

On 9 July, Berchtold discovered that Franz Joseph also approved of energetic action against Serbia. He was "worried that weak behavior would discredit our position vis-à-vis Germany." . . .

In order to overcome this opposition and delay in Vienna, German ambassador von Tschirschky . . . almost daily called at the Ballhausplatz. . . . While Tschirschky continued to point out threateningly that Berlin would interpret Austrian hesitation as a sign that the Great Power Austria-Hungary was resigning its position, the Foreign Office tried to reassure and to encourage the Austrian ambassador in Berlin, Szögyény, that the opportunity was uniquely favorable also for a war against France and Russia: on 12 July, Szögyény explained in a lengthy report why the emperor and the "German circles that count" were "one might almost say, forcing" their Austro-Hungarian ally "to take possibly even military action against Serbia." The German government regarded the present moment as "politically the right one" also from the German point of view.

> According to the German point of view, there are general political considerations and in particular factors resulting from the assassination at Sarajevo that speak for the choice of the present moment.

For, one is convinced [in Berlin] that Russia is arming for war and had "made direct provision for it in its calculations for the future, but was not planning it for the present moment, or put better, was not yet sufficiently prepared for it at the present moment." But should Russia decide nevertheless in favor of military intervention in behalf of Serbia,

> it is at present not nearly militarily ready or as strong as it is likely to be in a few years.

Moreover, the German government believed that it saw signs

> that at present, England would not take part in a war that started over a Balkan country, not even if it led to an armed clash with Russia, perhaps also with France. . . .

Tisza as well as Berchtold . . . concurrently informed Tschirschky that the handing over of the ultimatum would be postponed until 25 July. They stated that this delay had been decided upon so that delivery of the ultimatum would not proceed precisely while French president Poincaré was in Petersburg. . . .

Important preparations in case of mobilization were set afoot in all ministries in Berlin on 18 July. The preparations of the Great General Staff were already complete by then. On this day, the chancellor invited the Prussian ministers responsible [for mobilization] and secretaries of state of the Reich ministries for consultations under the chairmanship of the State Secretary of the Ministry of the Interior. "Guidelines for the treatment of Social Democrats, Poles, and Danes" were "to be prepared" immediately. Moreover, Bethmann Hollweg expressed the fervent hope that it would not be necessary to put the entire Empire on a war footing immediately upon proclamation of mobilization. . . . On 20 July, Delbrück, State Secretary of the Interior, accordingly fixed 24 July for the first meeting "on the limitation of the declaration of the state of war and other measures preliminary to mobilization." . . . [Bethmann Hollweg announced that it] was necessary to "emphasize the defensive war." In order to assure a united domestic front, it was essential that Russia was at all cost blamed for the coming conflict. Already now, on 23 July (that is, one day after the Austrian ultimatum had been delivered in Belgrade), the chancellor calculated on a Russian general mobilization in response to the Austrian measure:

> Should war break out, it will be the result of Russian mobilization ab irato, before possible negotiations. In that case, we can hardly remain calm and negotiate any longer because, if we are to have any chance of winning at all, we have to strike at once.

The Mediation Attempts of the European Concert of Nations

On Friday morning, the ultimatum delivered on Thursday afternoon (23 July) in Belgrade was published in the Viennese press, and on the same day it was handed to the governments in the European capitals by the Austro-Hungarian ambassadors. The news hit like a bomb, because almost four weeks had passed since the assassination [at Sarajevo], and hence the severity of the demands was all the more pronounced and less comprehensible. . . . British Foreign Secretary Grey immediately tried to mediate so that the conflict between Austria and Serbia would not erupt into a war between Austria and Russia, and thus into a European war. . . . But even though Grey had suggested mediation by the other Great Powers — not for the conflict between Austria and Serbia but only for a conflict between Austria and Russia — and had thus also wanted to "localize" the conflict, the German Foreign Office failed to respond to his suggestion — just as it had likewise rejected the request for an extension of the ultimatum to Serbia. . . .

The British Foreign Secretary continued his efforts to mediate in case of a threatening clash between Austria and Russia. . . . On Sunday, 26 July, Grey suggested a conference of the ambassadors of the noninvolved four powers in order to give Austria-Hungary satisfaction, and thereby to avoid a world war. Germany also rejected this proposal on the grounds that it could not haul Austria before a European court of justice. Instead, the German Foreign Office pointed out that channels already existed for a direct understanding between Petersburg and Vienna. On 27 July, Grey, during another conversation with Lichnowsky, for the first time voiced his suspicion that Germany was not seriously interested in mediation. . . .

Lichnowsky concluded his report with the observation that "all the world" in London was convinced

> that the key to the situation lies in Berlin, and that in case one seriously wanted peace there, one would be able to prevent Austria from pursuing, as Sir Grey puts it, a foolhardy policy. . . .

In reality, Bethmann Hollweg merely sent Lichnowsky's telegram on to Vienna — incidentally, without the concluding remarks — and appealed to the Vienna government to bear in mind Germany's difficult situation. The instruction to Tschirschky corresponded in content to the chancellor's letter to the emperor. It expressly emphasized that "we [Germany] must give the impression of being forced into the war." Lest the government in Vienna was still confused concerning the determination of its German ally, Jagow had summoned the Austrian ambassador and prepared him for possible British mediation proposals.

> The German government firmly guaranteed that it in no way identified itself with the proposals, that it in fact was decidedly opposed to

considering them, and that it was passing them on only in response to the British request. . . .

After Austria-Hungary had declared war on Serbia the next morning, 28 July, at Germany's urging, Berchtold officially rejected the British proposal with diplomatic courtesy on the grounds that

a state of war already exists between the Monarchy and Serbia at the very moment that Germany is making this move, and that the Serbian reply has therefore been overtaken by events.

The declaration of war on Serbia had been decided on 27 July for 28 or 29 July "primarily in order to knock the props out from under any attempt at intervention."

Even before this Austrian action against Serbia had made the outbreak of a European war still more likely, feverish activity had begun in the various ministries in Berlin. Moltke, Waldersee, and Tirpitz had returned to Berlin on 26 July, the emperor on 27 July. Immediately, on 26 July, Moltke had sent the Foreign Office the draft of the ultimatum to Belgium for examination and information. Mobilization orders even for civilian authorities were prepared for the emperor's signature. Admiral von Müller, upon returning from the North Sea cruise, summarized his impressions of the situation in Berlin as follows:

Tendency of our policy: stay calm, let Russia put itself in the wrong — but then, do not shy away from war.

The Austro-Hungarian naval attaché in Berlin had the same impression on this same 27 July. He wrote

that people here await all possible complications with utmost calm and regard the moment for a big settling of accounts as highly favorable.

Neither the Foreign Office nor the General Staff were thrilled with the emperor's early return because it was feared that Wilhelm II might disrupt the government's carefully planned concept with proposals of his own. In fact, these fears were realized; for, when the text of the Serbian reply was presented to the emperor — albeit, only on the morning of 28 July — he regarded this note as a Serbian "capitulation of the most humiliating kind" and decided: "Therewith, there no longer exists *any reason for war*." . . .

Crisis in Berlin: 29 and 30 July

The tension in Berlin reached its zenith in the late afternoon of 29 July. Following the Austrian declaration of war on Serbia and the shelling of Belgrade, the only news received was that of the partial mobilization of the four southern military districts — despite all the threats from Petersburg that Russia could not possibly accept the Austrian provocations with equanimity. The General Staff and the War Ministry urged that the critical gain in time should not be wasted, and insisted that a state of imminent war should be declared immediately. . . .

The . . . Saxon military plenipotentiary in Berlin . . . Leuckart reported to his government on the same day: he had heard from the minister of war that "nothing vital had been decided" so far at the Crown Council.

> *There is no doubt that the Chief of the General Staff favors war, whereas the Imperial Chancellor is holding back. General von Moltke is alleged to have said that we will never again find a moment as favorable as the present one, when neither France nor Russia have finished expanding their military.*

Leuckart came to the conclusion:

> *After all this, I believe — even if the situation can be described as more peaceful and less tense — that it will still come to a general war.*

The military, first and foremost the Chief of the General Staff, at this stage of the crisis thought exclusively in terms of the minute details of the military-strategic timetable [Schlieffen Plan]; Bethmann Hollweg, on the other hand, regarded the Russian publication of general mobilization as the indispensable prerequisite for corresponding measures by Germany. Russia needed officially to seize the initiative before Germany could launch a war against France and Russia. The argument on the afternoon and evening of 29 July concerned whether Russia's partial mobilization against Austria sufficed to provide Germany with the *casus foederis* in the eyes of the European public; it was not over any fundamental reservations on the part of the imperial chancellor regarding the decision taken in early July to launch the war at this given moment.

Bethmann Hollweg took the view that Russia's partial mobilization did not suffice to give Germany cause to activate its alliance commitments.

> *We must wait for this [that is, the* casus foederis*] because otherwise we will not have public opinion either here or in England on our side. . . .*

Despite Moltke's urgent plea that a state of imminent war be declared, Bethmann Hollweg managed to bring about a further delay on that evening of 29 July. . . .

At the Crown Council at Potsdam on the afternoon of 29 July, at which the proclamation of the state of imminent war was on the agenda, the question of English neutrality in this war was also discussed in detail. Wilhelm II was convinced that England would remain neutral. The English king had given this assurance to his brother, Prince Heinrich, who had just returned from England. The emperor brushed aside the doubts expressed by State Secretary Tirpitz, who was also present, with the comment: "I have the word of a king, that is enough for me." After Bethmann Hollweg's return from the Potsdam discussions, he attempted, probably under pressure from the military, which was urging that the military timetable be preserved, to reap the fruits of his many years' wooing of the English. He invited the English ambassador to the Chancery and offered him a German-British neutrality agreement for the impending war of Germany and Austria against Russia and France. In return, he extended to the English government the assurance that Germany would not violate France's territorial integrity. Bethmann Hollweg gave no firm reply to the ambassador's question concerning the French colonies.

Had Bethmann Hollweg known that at this very moment the Foreign Office was deciphering a report from Lichnowsky containing a clear warning from Grey that England could under no circumstances remain neutral if Germany attacked France, he undoubtedly would not have taken this step, which revealed the intentions of the German government.

Lichnowsky's news had an alarming effect in the Foreign Office, especially since the imperial chancellor had stuck his neck out so far in his talk with Goschen. But Lichnowsky's telegram did not alter the German government's decision to go to war. Given the power relationships in Berlin, the chancellor and the Foreign Office could not have gone back on the decision, even if they now had opted against war. To be sure, Bethmann Hollweg tried immediately, during the night of 29–30 July, to persuade the Austrian ally not to reject all offers of mediation too curtly. . . . In explaining this warning, which must have surprised his ally, Bethmann Hollweg stressed that while the German government was fully prepared to honor its alliance obligations, it refused "to be drawn by Vienna into a worldwide conflagration without regard for our advice." Should Vienna reject all offers of mediation, Germany and Austria-Hungary would face four Great Powers (England, Russia, France, Italy), in which case Germany would have to shoulder the main burden of the war on account of England's involvement.

These famous "world-on-fire-telegrams" were the reaction of Bethmann Hollweg and the Foreign Office to the news that the continental war that Germany had contemplated — without involving England — could not now be fought.

That same night, Moltke also sent a telegram to Vienna. He informed his Austrian colleague Conrad von Hötzendorf that Russian *partial* mobilization was no cause for German mobilization, but that Germany needed to wait for a state of war to exist between Russia and Austria-Hungary. Moltke gave the instruction: "Do not declare war on Russia, but await Russia's attack." The military and the political leadership were therefore unanimous in demanding that Austria-Hungary should under no circumstances appear as the aggressor, but that it be left to Russia to take the decisive step that would lead to war. . . .

On the morning of 30 July, Bethmann Hollweg drafted a telegram for Wilhelm II to send to the Tsar. Therewith, the chancellor sought to detail the likely consequences of Russian mobilization in order to make the Tsar responsible for all ensuing developments; Germany was presented as prepared to negotiate to the end. But the emperor, deeply embittered by the Russian partial mobilization of which he had not been informed until the morning of 30 July and by the "betrayal" of England, this "miserable lot of shopkeepers," had already firmly refused to continue his role as mediator. For this reason, Bethmann Hollweg appealed to Wilhelm II's vision as a statesman by prophesying that "this telegram will become an especially important document for history. " . . .

The suspenseful anticipation as to whether the German concept, according to which Russia would assume the role of aggressor, could still be realized, was reflected in a speech that Bethmann Holl-weg delivered as Prussian prime minister at a meeting of the Ministry of State at 5 P.M. Optimism and pessimism balanced each other therein. In a brief survey of the present political situation, he stressed Germany's efforts to bring about an understanding between the governments in Vienna and Petersburg; he emphasized German and English cooperation aimed at avoiding a European war, and the military measures of Russia and France that threatened the peace. Germany, on the other hand, had not yet declared the "state of imminent war" at his, the chancellor's, instigation, because this would make war inevitable. His disappointment over England's attitude was revealed once more when he skeptically noted that "the hope of England [was] equal to zero. England will probably take the side of the Dual Alliance." Even Italy's attitude was unpredictable. There was no counting on Rumania and Bulgaria.

On the other hand, Bethmann Hollweg reassured his Prussian ministerial colleagues about the nation's unity:

> The general mood in Germany is good (which was confirmed by all present). Nothing of substance was to be feared from Social Democracy and the Social Democratic party executive, as he had been led to conclude from his negotiations with the Reichstag deputy Südekum. A general strike . . . or sabotage were out of the question.

. . . Shortly after 9 P.M., Bethmann Hollweg, Moltke, and Falkenhayn held a meeting at which the military forced the decision that a state of "imminent danger of war" be proclaimed not later than the following noon, 31 July — a measure that in Germany inevitably brought mobilization with it. With this decision, which was taken before news of the Russian general mobilization had been received, Berlin had fixed the beginning of the war for the first days in August — in fact, even without the government having been driven to this by Russia's general mobilization. By postponing the mobilization for fifteen hours, the chancellor had at any rate gained time in which the Russian government might yet take a step that would put it in the wrong in the eyes of the world, and allow him to realize his original plan.

Around 11 P.M., the first rumors concerning the ordering of general mobilization in Russia arrived in Berlin. . . . The issue discussed at this meeting in Berlin, after receipt shortly before midnight of the first news concerning the Russian general mobilization, was German mobilization. The military demanded an immediate decision; Bethmann Hollweg, on the other hand, demanded that the mobilization be delayed until Russia had time to reject an ultimatum that Germany had given it. Quartermaster-General Waldersee wrote in a letter to Jagow of July 1926 concerning Moltke:

> With us, his collaborators until the outbreak of the war, he had stipulated that he only desired to bring about mobilization, for the war would then start of its own accord — a declaration by us would only do harm.

As Bethmann Hollweg has attested in a letter to Jagow of August 1919, Moltke had not only favored an immediate mobilization, but concurrently the start of military operations. But the chancellor's view prevailed; namely, that if military actions were to be taken without an announcement [of war], then there was no reason to issue an ultimatum to Belgium . . . and that otherwise — as he put it to Ballin — "he could not carry the Socialists with him."

Thus, even this night the chancellor once more managed to prevail against the military and to get a hearing for his arguments in favor of a perfect preparation for starting the war. The decision to proclaim the "state of imminent war" at noon on 31 July was upheld. The proclamation of German mobilization, on the other hand, was delayed for yet another day. First, an ultimatum to cease armed measures would have to be sent to Russia. Bethmann Hollweg was able to bring about this last postponement not least because his prophesy that Russia could be made to appear the aggressor seemed at last to be coming true.

Following this second meeting on 30 July, Moltke cabled the Austrian Chief of the General Staff the go-ahead:

> Wait for Russian mobilization; Austria must be preserved, must mobilize immediately against Russia, Germany will mobilize. Italy must be forced to honor its alliance obligations through compensations.

The Austro-Hungarian military attaché in Berlin at the same moment sent off a similar telegram after a discussion with Moltke. It contained the following additional demands:

> Reject any new moves by England to preserve the peace. Perseverance with the European war [is] the last means with which to preserve Austria-Hungary. Germany is definitely coming in.

Like Tschirschky, who had been given instructions to pass along to the Ballhausplatz, Conrad was now also instructed not to take further steps leading to mediation. Thus, there existed unanimity on this point between the political and the military leadership in Germany. These telegrams clearly spelled out that Germany demanded an Austro-Hungarian mobilization against Russia, relegating the Austrian war against Serbia to second place, precisely as Bethmann Hollweg demanded of Vienna the following afternoon: "We expect from Austria immediate *active* participation in the war against Russia." . . .

31 July/1 August: "Mood Brilliant" in Berlin

On the morning of Friday, 31 July, English ambassador Goschen delivered the English government's rejection of the German demand for neutrality. Not for a moment, Goschen informed the chancellor, had the English government considered the German proposal. England would not commit itself to stand idly by "while French colonies are taken away and France is beaten."

> From the material point of view, such a proposal is unacceptable because France could be so crushed as to lose her position as a Great Power and to become subject to German policy — without additional territory in Europe being taken from it.

Nor could the English government agree to bargain away its obligations and interests concerning Belgium's neutrality.

Bethmann Hollweg received this disclosure in silence. It appeared to the ambassador as if the chancellor was so preoccupied with the news concerning Russian military measures along the German border that he was unable immediately to comprehend the English response fully. . . . The chancellor was concerned to make it clear to the English government that Russia was responsible for the war and that Germany was only reacting to this provocation. . . .

When the Russian general mobilization was officially announced around noon and the Austrians concurrently proclaimed total mobilization, all military and diplomatic actions prepared in Berlin began to be implemented according to plan. The appeals to Vienna, to pretend to be willing to negotiate, had in fact been abruptly halted the previous night. That same morning, 31 July, Berlin did not raise the question of mediation anew, whereas feverish activity ensued in London, Petersburg, Paris, and even Vienna in a final attempt to prevent the outbreak of the great European war.

The "state of imminent war" was declared in Berlin at 1 P.M. Wilhelm II and Bethmann Hollweg justified these measures in solemn and pathetic addresses to the nation with the *leitmotif* that Russia had forced the war upon the German nation. . . .

At 3 P.M., Wilhelm II approved the text of the ultimatum to Russia and the "inquiry" to France.

The Bavarian ambassador, Lerchenfeld, that afternoon of 31 July sent his government a telegram report of laconic brevity on the situation in Berlin:

> *Two ultimata are currently in circulation: Petersburg 12 hours, Paris 18 hours. Petersburg inquiry into reasons for mobilization, Paris inquiry whether it will remain neutral. Naturally, both will be answered in the negative. Mobilization at the latest Saturday, 1 August, around midnight. Prussian General Staff look ahead to war with France with great confidence, expects to defeat France within four weeks; poor spirit, few howitzers, and inferior guns in the French army. . . .*

Around 7 P.M., Moltke cabled Conrad: "Will Austria leave Germany in the lurch?" In place of Germany's customary *Nibelungentreue* to Austria, there now appeared the demand for Austrian military help in a war of the German Empire. . . .

The chief of the press section of the Foreign Office, Hammann, on 1 August also gave the press the guideline that Russia's general mobilization was the factor responsible for starting the war. . . . The emperor and the German nation were [depicted as] determined opponents of preventative wars. Rather, Germany, in tandem with England, had tried unceasingly to find a peaceful solution.

> *Russia alone forces war upon Europe, which no one except Russia wanted; Russia alone must bear the full weight of responsibility.*

This guideline was consistently upheld in the German White Book at the outbreak of the war on 2 August, as well as in Bethmann Hollweg's Reichstag speech of 4 August.

The real state of affairs in Berlin circles, however, was radically different from the picture that Hammann tried to paint for the foreign press — of an emperor in despair because of the outbreak of the war and of a German government unhappy over the failure of peace negotiations. The Chief of the General Staff, Moltke, had pleasant memories of 1 August: "There prevailed, as the saying goes, a joyful atmosphere." And Admiral von Müller wrote in his diary on 1 August:

> *The morning papers carry the addresses of the emperor and the chancellor to the enthusiastic people assembled in front of the imperial palace, and the chancellor's residence, respectively. Mood brilliant. The government has skilfully managed to make us appear the attacked. . . .*

30 July/1 August: Uncertainty in Vienna

. . . On the morning of 31 July, the Joint Ministerial Council met in Vienna in order to discuss the English mediation proposal of 29 July (mediation by the Great Powers not directly involved) and to consider compensations for Italy. There was agreement at this session that it would be impossible to halt Austrian hostilities against Serbia. It would not suffice for Austria simply to occupy Belgrade without defeating the Serbian army, "even were Russia prepared to consent to this." But, at the suggestion of Hungarian minister president Tisza, it was decided not to reject the English proposal outright, but to agree to it on two conditions: namely, that operations against Serbia be continued, and that the Russian mobilization be halted. . . .

The session of the Ministerial Council is proof of the fact that Austria-Hungary was determined not to lose the opportunity, once it had been seized, for a thorough reckoning with Serbia, even at the risk that this could precipitate a European war. Indeed, since the early hours of this day, it had also been the urgent advice of the German ally not to bow to any mediation offers, but rather to proceed with the already launched venture. Nevertheless, Vienna was not yet firmly convinced of the inevitability of war with Russia, and therefore searched for a suitable opportunity to prevent Russia from intervening militarily in the Austro-Serbian war. In Conrad's telegram to Moltke on the evening of 31 July it still says: ". . . we are not sure yet whether Russia is merely threatening, and hence we could not allow ourselves to be diverted from the advance against Serbia." Conrad then added: "A totally different situation arises if Germany declares that it wishes to press the war *at once*. Request relevant notification." Even after the world war, Quartermaster-General Waldersee complained in a letter to Jagow: Austria had vacillated far too long; "people [in Vienna] still wished to avoid the armed clash with Russia. This was very damaging for us with regard to the opening of the war." . . .

"Bombs on Nürnberg" . . .

. . . In his speech to the Reichstag [on 4 August], the chancellor pilloried Russia as responsible for the war, certain of the anti-Russian mood that had been fomenting for months among the German public:

> *Russia has hurled the torch into the house. We are engaged in a war with Russia and France that has been forced upon us. . . .*

After listing the alleged French border violations by bombers, cavalry patrols, etc., which proved that France had attacked Germany, [the chancellor] justified the entry of German troops into Luxemburg and Belgium through reference to the state of emergency in which the German Empire found itself, and he closed his speech with the proclamation:

> *Our army is in the field, our fleet is ready for action — behind it stands the entire German Volk! — the entire German Volk (down to the Social Democrats) united to the last man!*

Of the two central goals of Bethmann's concept for a war against Russia and France, one was realized on 4 August: the Social Democrats' vote for war credits. . . . Bethmann Hollweg's other goal, to keep England neutral in this war, proved illusory that same day.

Shortly after the chancellor's speech, the British ambassador presented himself at the Chancery in order to hand over an ultimatum regarding Belgian neutrality. When Bethmann Hollweg and Jagow could offer no other explanation than the one they had previously given, Goschen, in accordance with his instructions, asked for his passports and declared that England regarded itself as being at war with Germany as of midnight, Central European time.

Wayne C. Thompson

In the Eye of the Storm: Kurt Riezler

Wayne C. Thompson of Virginia Military Institute has provided the first book-length study of Kurt Riezler, Chancellor Theobald von Bethmann Hollweg's young adviser during the July crisis of 1914. It is based on Riezler's long-withheld and only recently published diary, which was not available to Fritz Fischer in 1961. Given the high likelihood that Bethmann Hollweg's papers were either lost or destroyed, the Riezler material is critical for understanding the mood that prevailed in Berlin in the summer of 1914. It also offers an alternative to Fritz Fischer's portrayal of a deliberate German attempt to instigate war to gain world power and promote economic interests.

Riezler's diary entries immediately after July 5 and 6 indicate that he was neither present at the high level meetings where the crucial decisions were made on those days, nor was he with the chancellor. In the days before July 5 Bethmann Hollweg was at his estate in Hohenfinow outside of Berlin while Riezler remained in Berlin. Bethmann Hollweg traveled by rail to see the kaiser four times from June 29 to July 5, but it is unknown whether he saw Riezler during these short visits to Potsdam. Seldom did Riezler ever accompany the chancellor on official visits to the kaiser. Of course, it can be assumed that Riezler maintained telephone contact with the chancellor and that he continued to do paper work for him while the latter was absent. There is no question that Riezler . . . advised Bethmann on the political strategy and tactics which the chancellor himself then recommended or decided. Undoubtedly, some clues as to the advice which Riezler gave can be gotten from his prewar writings.

Andreas Hillgruber maintains that the German policy at this

Reprinted from *In the Eye of the Storm: Kurt Riezler and the Crises of Modern Germany* by Wayne C. Thompson, pp. 72–95, by permission of the University of Iowa Press. Copyright 1980 by University of Iowa Press.

time "corresponded to a definite political calculation which the chancellor had developed in constant close contact with Riezler." Hillgruber was referring, of course, to Riezler's theory of the calculated risk, but he does not indicate when this "definite political calculation" had been developed. Although there is no supporting documentary evidence, it is certainly possible that in 1913 Riezler had discussed with the chancellor some of the arguments he made in *Grundzüge der Weltpolitik*, including that concerning the calculated risk. Also, although Riezler does not mention it in his diary, it is possible that they discussed Riezler's calculated risk argument, even if only by telephone, in the days before the Potsdam "Crown Council" and that the theory formed part of the general conceptual basis for the chancellor's approach to the crisis. It is true that the chancellor, as well as Riezler, strongly felt that the growing Serbian threat to Austria-Hungary was ultimately a serious threat to Germany's own vital interests. It is also true that, in contrast to previous Balkan crises, both sensed that the time had come for a bolder policy, even at the risk of a local war or, if unavoidable, a continental war in order to achieve a diplomatic realignment in the Balkans and thereby to reverse the steady deterioration of Germany's diplomatic and military position. . . . Further, we know from Riezler's diary entries that throughout the July crisis, the chancellor and his young assistant rationalized German support of Austria-Hungary since July 5 and 6 in terms of the possible diplomatic realignment which could flow from that policy. Indeed, the kind of favorable outcome resulting from a calculated risk such as Riezler described in *Grundzüge der Weltpolitik* would have been the optimal outcome of the July crisis, from the chancellor's point of view. . . .

On July 6 Riezler returned to Hohenfinow with Bethmann Hollweg, and that evening he was given a report of the situation by the chancellor. What Riezler heard surprised him greatly and seemed so important that he resumed his diary the next day for the first time since the second Moroccan crisis:

> Yesterday I drove out with the chancellor. The old castle, the wonderful gigantic lindens, the avenues like a Gothic arch. . . . In the evening on the veranda under the darkened sky a long conversation on the situation. The secret news which he tells me gives an unnerving picture. He views the Anglo-Russian negotiations concerning a naval agreement . . . with great concern, the last link in the chain. Lichnowsky is

much too gullible. He allows himself to be taken in by the English. Russia's military power growing rapidly; with the strategic extension into Poland the situation is untenable. Austria increasingly weaker and immobile; the undermining from the North [Poland] and Southeast has advanced very far. In any case incapable [for Austria] to go to war as our ally over a German problem. The Entente knows that; as a result, we are completely paralyzed.

I was completely horrified. I had not viewed the situation as being so bad. . . . The chancellor speaks of difficult decisions. The murder of Franz Ferdinand. Official Serbia involved. Austria wants to get right to work. The message of Franz Joseph to the kaiser with the questions concerning casus foederis. Our old dilemma with every Austrian Balkan action. If we encourage them, then they say we pushed them into it; if we discourage them, then it is said we left them in the lurch. Then they go to the Western powers, whose arms are open, and we lose the last reasonable ally. . . . An action against Serbia can lead to a world war. From a war, regardless of the outcome, the chancellor expects a revolution of everything that exists. That which exists has long outlived itself, is wholly without ideas. . . . Generally, delusion all around, a thick fog over the people. The same in all of Europe. The future belongs to Russia, which grows and grows and thrusts itself on us as a heavier and heavier nightmare. . . .

Riezler continued in July 8.

If the war comes from the East, so that we go to war for Austria and not Austria for us, then we have the prospect of winning it. If the war does not come, if the tsar does not want it, or if a perplexed France counsels peace, then we still certainly have the prospect of maneuvering the Entente apart over this matter.

These entries give insights into Bethmann's and Riezler's attitudes and roles during the July crisis. . . . We see in his scornful remarks about Lichnowsky the first indications of a serious miscalculation concerning Britain's stake in a potential European war. We see Riezler's concern about the steady decline in Austria's strength and his exaggerated anxiety about the possibility of Germany's losing her last ally if firm support were not granted to Austria. . . .

Riezler's remarks reveal a deep pessimism about the chance for Germany and Austria to resist an ever-expanding Russia. His concern about Russia was considerably less than Bethmann Hollweg's. The chancellor's strong feelings about the inevitability of Russian expansion were perhaps best shown by a remark which he made to Hans von Flotow, Germany's ambassador to Rome at the time of the outbreak: Bethmann Hollweg, "looking out over the park on his estate at Hohenfinow doubted whether there were any purpose in planting new trees because the Russians would be there in a few years anyway."

Both Bethmann Hollweg and Riezler knew from the beginning that an Austrian action against Serbia could lead to a world war. . . . However, in the eyes of German leaders there appeared to be no alternative to their policy of allowing Austria to deal harshly with Serbia at this time. Certainly no policy which would have resulted in a significant weakening of Austria-Hungary would have been acceptable to Germany. . . . No policy would have been acceptable which would have allowed Russia to strengthen herself greatly in the Balkans. . . . Bethmann Hollweg's fatalism regarding Russian expansion was not so great that he would have passively accepted a sudden and dramatic increase of Russian influence in the Balkans. . . . Riezler's pessimism about Germany's situation and about the chances to maintain peace continued to grow. "Our situation is terrible." The lack of control over events gave Riezler a feeling of helplessness.

As the prospect of war became more real, his mind dared to ponder the positive aspects of a war. "If the war should come and the veil [of friendliness which covers the real enmity among peoples] should fall, then the entire *Volk* will follow, driven by a sense of emergency and danger. Victory is liberation." His use of the words "emergency and danger" indicated that he was thinking primarily of "liberation" from the "*cauchemar des coalitions*," from the encirclement of which he wrote in *Grundzüge der Weltpolitik.* There is no question that Riezler hoped that the Austro-Serbian crisis would loosen or break some of the ties which existed among Britain, France, and Russia. However, he reflected upon another aspect of a war which he discussed with the chancellor: The "liberation" from petty things, the adventure of being a part of a great movement. "The chancellor thinks that I am too young not to be lured by the uncertain, the new, the great movement. For him the action is a leap into darkness and this [is] the gravest obligation." . . .

Riezler wrote on July 20 that "a very serious mood" prevailed in Berlin. "A heavy blanket of open sadness and of the greatest responsibility hangs over the men and over all conversations, broken only here and there by the children's need for gaiety. The chancellor is determined and taciturn."

Riezler's diary entries during the remainder of the crisis indicate an increasing apprehension about Russia; he even considered meeting this growing danger by reaching an agreement with Russia. He wrote on July 20 of

> . . . *Russia's growing claims and enormous explosive force. Uncontainable in a few years, especially if the present European constellation remains. If successful in changing it [constellation] or in loosening it up, then one must consider whether and how the entire present alliance system must be overturned and changed. But whether that is possible? . . .*

Riezler began on July 23, the day the Austrian ultimatum was delivered, to question whether Austria-Hungary should be supported at all and whether an alliance with Russia might have served German interests better. . . . Riezler no longer believed in the "vitality" of the Austro-Hungarian state. He wrote:

> *It is certainly characteristic for the entire political mess in Austria, which does not let go of the inherited lures of a world power, but which cannot even begin to maintain itself. We will certainly squat behind this weak state and will squander our youthful strength on the postponement of its disintegration. . . .*

On July 23 the political situation seemed very uncertain and mysterious to Riezler.

> *Sat and strolled for a long time under the great linden trees and reflected on everything. What will happen? Will the German Volk be saved or will it perish? Nature unconscious and unconcerned. . . . greater than the greatest event.*

On July 23, at 6:00 P.M., the Austrian ambassador in Belgrade, Wladimir Baron Giesl, presented the Austrian ultimatum to the Serbian government. . . . This ultimatum transformed the local quarrel into a world crisis. . . . It was still hoped in Berlin that the war could be localized. Nevertheless, as Riezler's entry on July 25 shows, the military, economic, and diplomatic preparations for a possible war with France and Russia were being made by Germany before the invasion of Serbia had begun:

> *Almost the entire time the last few days the chancellor has been on the telephone. Apparently preparations for every eventuality, talks with the military about which nothing is said. Merchant marine is warned. Havenstein financial mobilization. Until now nothing could be made which would be conspicuous. Great movement.*

Without question Riezler, along with the chancellor's other aides, was deeply involved with these economic and diplomatic preparations for an eventual war. . . .

The philosophic Riezler pondered the meaning of this confusion and uncertainty. "What does fate want? But fate is mostly stupid and unconscious and muddled in many coincidences. Whoever takes hold of it has it." Riezler believed that individual human action could help control events. Nevertheless, he continued to see difficulties. Fate "in this cursed, confused modern world has become so multifarious, can neither be calculated nor comprehended. Too many factors at the same time." . . . Riezler was in complete agreement with Bethmann Hollweg, who . . . saw "a fate greater than human power lying over the European situation and over our people."

The excitement in Germany on the evening of July 25 showed that the crisis was approaching a peak. Arriving in Berlin, Riezler observed:

> *Movement on the streets. Crowds of people in Unter den Linden waiting for the Serbian answer. . . . However, the people have not yet been awakened fully from the dream of peace, which they still take for granted, still disbelieving, amazed and curious.*

There was an air of excitement in Berlin which Riezler detected at this critical point:

> *In the evening and on Sunday people singing. At first the chancellor thought that only juveniles were taking advantage of the opportunity for racket and excitement and were letting their curiosity run wild. However, there is more and more of this, and the tones are becoming more genuine. In the end the chancellor is deeply moved, deeply stirred. . . . In the people an enormous, if confused, urge to act, a yearning for a great movement, to rise up for a great movement, to rise up for a great cause, to show one's ability.*

Bethmann Hollweg had reason to be pessimistic because on July 27 the crisis entered its most serious stage. Riezler recorded on this day that "all reports point to war." Austria decided to declare war on Serbia. . . . Riezler correctly identified the critical points: Russia and London. He reported "obviously hard struggles over mobilization in St. Petersburg." On July 26 and 27 the German Foreign Office received reports from Germany's ambassador in St. Petersburg, Pourtalès, of Russia's partial mobilization. . . . Riezler also observed that "England's language has changed," and indeed it had. On July 26 and 27 Lichnowsky sent Berlin four telegrams . . . warning Berlin against believing that a war between Serbia and Austria could be localized. . . .

Britain's new hostile attitude changed the atmosphere in Berlin. Riezler writes that there was "hectic activity in the Chancellery. No one sleeps any more. I see the chancellor only for seconds. He is entirely changed, has not a single minute to ponder and for that reason is fresh, active, lively, and relaxed." . . . From July 27 events went so rapidly that in a meeting of the Prussian State Ministry in the afternoon of July 30, Bethmann Hollweg had to admit that "all governments including Russia's and the great majority of the peoples are basically peaceful, but all direction is lost and the stone has begun to roll." . . .

The chancellor's last minute efforts to stop the development toward general war were doomed by another powerful influence at Berlin — the voice of military necessity. He informed the Prussian Ministry of State on July 30 that "we have lost control." Military aspects had become overriding after reports of Russia's partial mobilization had arrived in Berlin. . . . On the thirtieth Moltke openly advocated full mobilization of German forces. . . . At 9:00 P.M., on the evening of the thirtieth, . . . Falkenhayn and Moltke were successful in gaining Bethmann Hollweg's agreement "that by noon of the next day at the latest, a decision concerning the proclamation of the state of imminent danger must be reached." . . .

Did Bethmann Hollweg or Riezler see the political danger in the German plans for troop deployment, known as the Schlieffen Plan? Before December 1912, they were not even aware that such a plan existed. Although the military updated these plans annually, no war council was ever held during Bethmann Hollweg's chancellorship at which military plans were discussed with political leaders. The isolation of military thinking from politics was characteristic of Wilhelmine Germany, and during the war Riezler bitterly remarked that "the concept of the purely military is celebrating orgies." However, there is no evidence whatsoever that either the chancellor or Riezler at any time objected to the Schlieffen Plan or were concerned about its negative consequences. . . . Bethmann Hollweg publicly confessed that the German invasion of Belgium was an "injustice," but he claimed that necessity had forced Germany to commit this injustice, which "we will make good as soon as our military goal has been attained."

Despite his realization that the violation of Belgium was an injustice, the chancellor could not believe, as he confessed to British Ambassador Goschen in an emotional encounter on August 4, that Britain would go to war against a friendly nation "just for a scrap of paper" — for Belgian neutrality. In his memoirs Bethmann Hollweg admitted that "a scrap of paper" had been a very unwise choice of words. . . .

Riezler's diary is the closest and most complete immediate account of the German leaders' thinking during the July crisis. . . . His diary indicates that from the beginning, not merely at the end of the crisis, German leaders recognized the possibility that Britain would side with France and Russia and that the local war could expand into a European or world war. Riezler and Bethmann Hollweg were willing to risk such a world war although both hoped that the Austro-Serbian war could be localized. . . . However, their desire to weaken or split the Entente was great, and they believed that this could have been accomplished through the humiliation of Serbia and through French refusal to support Russian policy. . . .

Riezler's diary reveals no deliberate attempt on the part of the leading German policymakers to start a war either to establish German hegemony in Europe or to clear a path for German territorial annexations. Both the chancellor and Riezler were convinced, however, of the necessity to support Austria-Hungary in order to maintain Germany's position as a world power. Neither saw any realistic alternative to supporting Austria. There is no indication that "monopoly capitalists," industrialists, or any economic motives played a significant role in the decisions made in Berlin during July. Security considerations were foremost in their minds.

Based on Riezler's diary entries during the July crisis, direct pressure from nationalist groups had little or no influence on the chancellor's decisions. Nor was the chancellor decisively influenced by parliamentary leaders, newspaper owners, editors, and financiers. Bethmann Hollweg never capitulated easily to public opinion and to parliamentary and industrial pressure. . . .

Finally, Riezler's entries reveal a certain measure of fatalism which crept into his and the chancellor's minds. Riezler saw events slipping out of human control. They also reveal no trace of criticism of the chancellor's policy during the July crisis. Once war was unavoidable, Riezler showed enthusiasm and optimism. Though he criticized Austrian conduct during the crisis, he wrote that "it is just as well. The [German] *Volk* is indestructible. It may suffer defeats, but they can be turned into blessings if it is clever." With peace no longer possible, Riezler set about to help achieve German victory.

Wolfgang Kruse

War Euphoria in Germany in 1914

Wolfgang Kruse's critical analysis, *War and National Integration: A New Interpretation of the Social Democratic "Civil Truce," 1914–1915*, is a revised version of his 1990 Berlin Technical University dissertation. In this selection, he argues that the "war euphoria" of 1914 rested mainly with middle-class professionals and students and that "depression, frustration, and fear" dominated working-class quarters. Finally, Kruse, a professor at Hagen University, Germany, warns against analyzing this "euphoria" simplistically along gender lines.

Few historical conceptions have experienced such general dissemination as the belief that the overwhelming majority of the populace in the German Empire welcomed the First World War with enthusiastic, nationalistic prowar fervor. The deep embodiment of this conception in the consciousness of professional historians as well as of

From Marcel van der Linden and Gottfried Mergner, eds. *Kriegsbegeisterung und mentale Kriegsvorbereitung. Interdisziplinäre Studien.* Reprinted by permission of Duncker & Humblot GmbH, Berlin. Translated by Holger H. Herwig.

the interested public runs up against the hard reality of a lack of empirical research into the mood and the behavior of the populace at the start of the war. . . .

1. The Contextual Origins of the War Euphoria

The historical sources make clear time and again that the actual war must have acted as a release [from pressure and fear]. But there is ground for great skepticism with regard to the widely held notion that it brought about the much-sought-after liberation from a banal and empty peace through the cleansing adventure of war. A few frustrated intellectuals — such as the often-cited writers Georg Heym and Thomas Mann — may in fact have desired war and hailed its outbreak for this reason, but not the great majority of the populace, which viewed the war even in its very beginning stages with distance and rejection.

To be sure, immediately after the publication of the Austro-Hungarian ultimatum to Serbia on 25 July, there were prowar demonstrations in many cities of the German Empire that for the most part were undertaken by students and other elements of the so-called "best and better social classes." But, in fact, of far greater importance for any assessment of the general mood of the populace before the outbreak of war are the Social Democratic antiwar gatherings and demonstrations, which also were held already in the last week of July. And although they were not widely publicized, they nevertheless demonstrated far greater mass participation with their three-quarters of a million people. The [SPD paper] *Vorwärts* thus could justifiably claim on 29 July: "The absurd swindle that the majority of people were seized by war euphoria, was . . . thoroughly discredited by the working class."

Nor was this prowar sentiment discernably dominant at this time in middle-class circles. After a "war of songs" had broken out during the previous night in Berlin's inner city between Social Democratic and chauvinistic demonstrators, both of whom had tried to drown the other out with their songs, the conservative Berlin daily paper *Die Post* at least noted with bitter disappointment: "Only a small part of the tens of thousands who paraded up and down [Unter den] Linden was patriotically minded, or dared to bear witness to this feeling."

The constantly conjured-up feeling of release apparently was not caused by a direct wish to charge off to war. Still, how could this feeling of distance and rejection on the part of the majority of the populace transform itself within a few days into obvious war euphoria?

The throngs of humanity that poured into the inner cities in the last days of July were spurred on above all else by a need to obtain information. In a society that knew neither radio nor television, the special newspaper editions and cablegrams distributed by the newspaper bureaus were the only means of obtaining the latest news about the course of the European crisis, which conjured up the danger of world war. The Social Democratic *Fränkische Tagespost* accordingly described the events that took place in Nürnberg's inner city on 25 and 26 July as follows:

> *The number of people out in the streets grows steadily. In front of the newspaper offices, in front of the Austro-Hungarian Consulate, they crowd together into a huge throng. They await cablegrams, special editions. . . . Finally the first telegram appears in a window display. What will it bring? They all press forward. Quickly their eyes scan the few sheets. Then they are off to spread the news. . . . Soon the streets fill up once again. The throng, which constantly grows larger, flows up and down the inner city. Then the first special editions appear. Hungrily they are devoured by eager eyes. . . . Throughout the entire morning, over the noon break, through the afternoon, and well into the evening, [there is] the same lively scene in the city. The throng surges and recedes, but it never disappears completely. No one wants to miss a single telegram.*

In fact, initially we are dealing less with war euphoria than with a growing excitement that grips the insecure masses. *Vorwärts* somewhat later summarizes the situation in Berlin as follows:

> *Rising and falling streams of humanity covered Berlin's streets during these days. And anyone who still maintained a drop of calm blood, despite these momentous events, had to call on his last ounce of energy in order not be be sucked into the excitement that was rising hour by hour. It was as if a single all-embracing notion had captured all hearts and minds. . . . And the minute that this sea of humanity in Berlin threatened for only a minute to recede here and there, a new flood rolled in, carried by the special editions with their alarming reports, with which the press flooded the streets.*

This prowar propaganda spread not only the ideology of a defensive war. It also galvanized the mounting excitement into an almost unbearable tension. As the future Communist Karl Grünberg accurately explained, there developed "an atmosphere of great anxiety, of a horror without end, one in which the horrible end would literally have to be seen as release [from fear and horror]." The conservative paper *Tägliche Rundschau* accordingly described the reaction of the waiting masses to the declaration of a threatening state of war and the proclamation of a domestic state of siege in Berlin on 31 July as follows: "Well, finally! It goes through the masses like a cry of release. No merry-making can be heard, no cheers arise, all countenances are serious — the ghastly tension that has gripped Berlin is released in one liberating breath: So, after all!"

But the war had not definitely begun with that; the tension began to mount anew. Gustav Roethe, professor of German philology at Berlin's Friedrich-Wilhelm University, later determined the mood of the following day, 1 August 1914, thusly: "But the tension still brooded; we still waited, and doubted, and stared at one another with silent, serious questions. Then finally the release, the announcement of mobilization. . . ."

Since the preceding years had already stood under the crushing imprint of a constantly mounting threat of war, this sense of release — as the Free-Protestant *Christliche Welt* stressed — now allowed the "really horrible war" to appear "as a blessing after years of tension." . . .

2. The Limits of the War Euphoria

In the final analysis, ideologically determined prejudices lay at the root of the belief in a general, nationalistic war euphoria. As can be demonstrated, for example, by the wildly exaggerated numbers [up to 1 million] and highly glorified reports of war volunteers, from the very start of the war [official circles and the media] drew with decidedly propagandistic intentions an idealized picture of the alleged euphoric spirit of sacrifice on the part of the populace. This propagandistic stereotype has basically molded the public's consciousness about the First World War until today. Not just the heroizing of the war on the part of the nationalistic right during the Weimar·Republic and throughout National Socialism has largely led to the perpetuation [of this consciousness]. But also the Social Democratic rejection of the Marxist-Leninist thesis of [the SPD's alleged] treason against the workers has advanced the overemphasis on war euphoria [in 1914]. And, last but not least, [this stereotype] also contains preconceptions of irrationalism and fanaticism on the part of the masses — a topos that especially intellectuals, who write the history, have taken to heart.

The principal criticism to be raised against this dominant ideological tradition is that its narrow research base up to now has not permitted generalizations about the mood and the behavior of the populace in the German Empire at the start of the war. Any new intensive investigations will first have to abandon the well-trodden paths of this traditional historiography and return to the sources. Beyond that, it will be necessary to differentiate by societal categories such as class, gender, religious denomination, region, age, and political affiliation. Initial critical investigations into this ideologically based historiography allow us to conjecture with some certainty that the reaction to the start of the war by Social Democratic workers, but also by countless other people, in no way was akin to the picture of a general, nationalistic euphoria developed by the media. For example, the Danish Reichstag deputy Hans Peter Hanssen, having recently read on the train to Berlin press reports about the alleged dominant euphoria in the capital, on 2 August noted with surprise in his diary: "The opposite is evidently the truth, judging by what I have had ample opportunity to see on the way here to the hotel."

Depression, frustration, and fear were the sentiments that right at the start of the war gripped many, apparently even the majority, of people. None of these [sentiments] were published, but rather were suppressed. The young Hamburg Social Democrat Wilhelm Heberlein noted in his diary after the announcement of mobilization on 1 August: "Most of the people were depressed, as if they were to be beheaded the next day." His comrade in Bremen, Wilhelm Eildermann, that same day added his own impression: "The most low-spirited mood that I have ever witnessed prevails. Mothers, women, and brides and the usual attendants bring the young men to the trains and cry. All have the feeling that the [men] are going straight to the slaughterhouse."

Not only the Social Democrats expressed such sentiments. A

Protestant pastor from a farming community in Württemberg somewhat later reported as follows: "No one made his way forward in
these days and under this pressure of the New with a sense of excitement — other than it was brought on by alcohol, and even of this
one saw only a few, soon vanishing exceptions." Another pastor from
a workers' village near Frankfurt am Main described the mood there
in these terms: "All the village was filled with sorrow during the last
week of July. With the onset of mobilization, when the last thread of
hope for peace was severed, it grew even stiller and despair set in. No
euphoria, no patriotic songs." The Social Democratic *Volkswille* in
Hanover probably justifiably concluded on 8 August 1914 that in
Germany, "massive depression reigned in broad circles of the populace in the days in which the state of war was declared, the mobilization of troops was ordered, and the declarations of war rolled off the
assembly line."

In the days that followed, the material misery of large segments
of the populace occasioned by the war set narrow bounds to the
euphoria in short order. Panicked reactions already in the development phase of the war had led to long lines in front of banks and
shops. After the start of the war, the fears that led to hoarding were
exacerbated and soon were surpassed in intensity by a rapid increase
in unemployment, food price hikes, and insufficient social-service
support for the families of those called to the colors. To be sure,
even in the workers' sections of Berlin one could be surprised by victory celebrations and trooping of the national colors in the wake of
the first victory bulletins from the front; but already the first public-
opinion reports by the police on 22 August 1914 from the proletarian
sections in the north and east of the capital simultaneously soberly
noted that the general mood of the populace was rather depressed.
And a pastor from the working-class area of Moabit opined: "The
real euphoria — I should say, the euphoria among the educated, who
seem to think that they can afford it, and who do not suffer from
impending food shortages — seems to me to be missing. The people
truly think very rationally, and misery weighs heavily upon them."

A diary entry by Wilhelm Heberlein on 16 August once more
reveals how depressing the reality of everyday life was for many people, especially in August 1914, and the despondency that reigned in
many households: "I have to collect the party dues because many of
the comrades have been drafted — miserable living quarters, [the]

sadness of many of the women left behind, unemployment, dejection, people accepting a life alone." We are in no way dealing here with a picture that applied only to SPD members. Even Johanna Boldt, a Hamburg merchant dealing in colonial goods who initially had been gripped by the war euphoria and who thereafter remained nationalistically minded, at the end of October wrote to her husband at the front: "If only this horrible war would just end! The people wish for nothing so much as for an end to this wretched war."

Undoubtedly, it would be very interesting to investigate the specific gender differences in how people viewed the war. But one has to warn against presupposing differing degrees of support for the war on the part of men and women. Women on the "home front" could also get excited about the war, while the actual war experiences of the men [at the front] especially were hardly designed to foster euphoria. To the degree that this [euphoria] existed at all even at the start of the war, it found a quick end at the latest when confronted with the realities of the war. Already on 15 September 1914, the Social Democratic *Schwäbische Tagwacht* summarized the contents of the first letters from the front thusly: "Due to reasons of military censorship, it is impossible to reproduce all the horrors of the war. Many of these are only alluded to. But in all letters there suddenly and without warning crops up time and again as a warning cry: the war is something horrible!" . . .

Neither the often-touted adventure of "trench camaraderie" nor the romanticized reproduction of Ernst Jünger's *Storm of Steel* in reality corresponded to the dominant experiences of the majority of soldiers.

D. C. B. Lieven

Russia Accepts a General War

Dominic Lieven, lecturer in government at the London School of Economics and Political Science, concludes after an exhaustive study of Russian and Soviet archives that neither Imperial Russia's minister in Belgrade (N. V. Hartwig) nor its military attaché (Colonel V. I. Artamonov) had any foreknowledge of the conspiracy to murder Archduke Francis Ferdinand; responsibility for the regicide rests fully with Serbian military intelligence. However, Lieven argues that Russia's "historic mission" and "prestige in the Balkans" permitted no other policy than to take a firm stand. Thus, Lieven agrees with Luigi Albertini that by adopting a hard line, St. Petersburg made a European conflict probable.

There is no reason to suspect that Petersburg had any foreknowledge of the conspiracy which led to the murder of the Austrian heir-apparent though it is conceivable that Hartwig and Artamonov knew of the plot. . . . Russian documents published by the Soviet government do not prove that Hartwig and Artamonov knew nothing of the conspiracy. On the other hand they do illustrate that both men were unsympathetic to the Black Hand's struggle against Pašic and were well aware that Serbia needed a long respite before running the risks of involvement in any further external crises. Unless reliable evidence shows the contrary, one must therefore assume that neither Hartwig nor Artamonov would have lent any support to a conspiracy which could not fail to exacerbate Austro-Serb relations.

The Russian government's ignorance about the conspiracy played an important role in the July crisis. It is now known that although the conspirators were Young Bosnians fired by their own hatred of Vienna's policy, they were armed and smuggled across the

Austrian frontier by Serbian officials who knew and sanctioned their intentions. Moreover, that sanction came from the head of Serbian military intelligence, Dimitrijević [Apis], and may well have been connected in a roundabout fashion with his own desire to topple Pašic, the prime minister. The fact that the Serb government could not control its own army or nationalists only in part diminishes its responsibility for the murder; indeed, . . . such a situation strengthened the case for Austrian intervention to crush the otherwise uncontrollable radical and nationalist hydra. As Apis' nephew later wrote, had his uncle's role in the conspiracy been revealed in July 1914 this "would have done untold harm to his country." . . . Had the truth been known about the conspiracy it is possible that Sazonov would have from the outset of the crisis been more willing to compromise with Vienna, while the revulsion against Serbia in London would have been very great. As it was, however, the Austrians neither discovered the link with Apis nor actually communicated their dossier of evidence to Petersburg. Sazonov was therefore faced with unproven Austrian statements about Serbian involvement in the conspiracy which, given Vienna's past history of basing anti-Serb claims on false documents, he rightly regarded with great suspicion. . . .

Although during the first three weeks of July 1914 the Russians were alarmed at times by reports of impending harsh Austrian action in Belgrade they were reassured by firm Austrian statements that such rumours were untrue. When the crisis broke on 24 July the Russians therefore felt gulled and were taken by surprise. This increased their distrust of Vienna and meant that for much of the last week in July Russia was represented by chargés d'affaires in Paris, Berlin, Vienna and Belgrade, the three ambassadors being on holiday. . . . Danilov, the Quartermaster-General, was also on leave and the absence from Petersburg of the General Staff's strongest personality and leading expert on mobilisation was to have important results.

On receiving the text of the ultimatum at 10 A.M. on 24 July Sazonov . . . "considered war unavoidable." Immediately reporting, for the first time ever, on the telephone to Nicholas, Sazonov stated that given the ultimatum's demands and its brutal wording Austria must know that it "could not be complied with by Serbia" and must therefore be intending to attack her neighbour. It was obvious, said

Sazonov, that such an ultimatum could not have been sent without German consent, which strongly suggested that the Central Powers were intending to use their present military superiority to start a European war. Calmer and less pessimistic than his Foreign Minister, Nicholas ordered the Council of Ministers to discuss Russia's response to the ultimatum.

Before the Council's meeting, which took place in the afternoon of 24 July, Sazonov discussed the crisis with the British and French ambassadors. Paléologue urged a tough line and promised Sazonov unequivocal French support. With his President and Prime Minister very difficult to contact on the battleship *France* a great burden rested on Paléologue's shoulders but although nothing precise or detailed is known about Russo-French discussions during Poincaré and Viviani's visit to Russia in July 1914 one can only assume that the ambassador's self-confidently vigorous line echoed the approach taken by his country's leaders in the previous week. It was, in any event, in accord with France's diplomatic stance over the previous eighteen months. Buchanan, as one would expect, was far more non-committal and urged Sazonov to gain the maximum time possible in which diplomacy might find a peaceful solution to the crisis.

Russia's response to the Austrian move was decided at a meeting of the Council of Ministers which began at 3 P.M. and lasted for over two hours. Given the crucial importance of this meeting it is worth studying in some detail the statements of Russia's ministers on the afternoon of 24 July. Sazonov spoke first. He stressed Germany's

> *systematic preparations, which were calculated to increase her power in Central Europe in order to enable her to carry out her wishes, not only as regards matters in the Near East, but in all international questions, without taking into consideration the opinion and influence of the powers not included in the Triple Alliance.*

In the course of the last decade Russia had shown great moderation and made many concessions wherever her interests and Berlin's came into conflict but "Germany had looked upon our concessions as so many proofs of our weakness and far from having prevented our neighbours from using aggressive methods, we had encouraged them." Now had to come the moment to make a stand. The Austrian ultimatum to Belgrade was beyond question drawn up with German connivance and would if accepted turn Serbia into a *de facto* protectorate of the Central Powers. In the past Russia had "made immense sacrifices" to secure the independence of the Slav peoples and if she now abandoned under threat "her historic mission, she would be considered a decadent state and would henceforth have to take second place among the powers," losing "all her authority" and allowing "Russian prestige in the Balkans" to "collapse utterly." . . . A firm stand would, however, mean a real risk of war with the Central Powers, whose consequences were all the more dangerous "since it was not known what attitude Great Britain would take in the matter."

Next to speak was Krivoshein, the Minister of Agriculture. . . . Krivoshein was the most powerful figure in the Russian government. His success in administering the vital and complicated programme of agrarian reforms, together with his clear mind, simple manner and political skill had won him the full confidence of Nicholas II, which gave him a considerable influence in the state's overall internal and external policy. Peter Bark, the Minister of Finance, records that on the afternoon of 24 July Krivoshein's "declaration was the most instrumental in influencing our decisions."

The Minister of Agriculture stated that only the army's loyalty had saved the régime from collapse in 1905. Since then a constitutional system had been established, Russia's financial position vastly improved and major reforms in the armed forces undertaken. "However, our rearmament programme had not been completed and it seemed doubtful whether our Army and our Fleet would ever be able to compete with those of Germany or Austro-Hungary [sic] as regards modern technical efficiency," since in cultural and industrial terms Russia was far behind the Central Powers.

> On the other hand, general conditions had improved a great deal in Russia in the past few years and public and parliamentary opinion would fail to understand why, at the critical moment involving Russia's vital interests, the Imperial Government was reluctant to act boldly. . . . No one in Russia desired war. The disastrous consequences of the Russo-Japanese War had shown the grave danger which Russia would run in case of hostilities. Consequently, our policy should aim at reducing the possibility of a European war [but] if we remained passive we would not attain our object. . . . In his view stronger language than we had used hitherto was desirable. All factors tended to prove that the most judicious policy Russia could follow in present circumstances was a return to a firmer and more energetic attitude towards the unreasonable claims of the Central-European powers.

In private conversation after the session Krivoshein added that although the policy he advocated entailed "serious risks," the latter would not be reduced by a conciliatory stance. "He thought that the only hope of influencing Germany was to show them, by making a firm stand, that we had come to the end of the concessions we were prepared to make. In any case, we should take all the steps which would enable us to face an attack."

Bark, the Minister of Finance, records that "Krivoshein's speech made a profound impression on the Cabinet." Goremykin then turned to the service ministers for their views. Sukhomlinov and Grigorovich stated that although great improvements in the armed forces had occurred since 1905, the programme of rearmament was not completed and Russian military superiority over the Central Powers could not be assumed. "They stated nevertheless that hesitation was no longer appropriate as far as the Imperial Government was concerned. They saw no objection to a display of greater firmness in our diplomatic negotiations." . . . The other ministers also "shared the opinion of Sazonov and Krivoshein," and Goremykin summed up by saying "that it was the Imperial Government's duty to decide definitely in favour of Serbia"; that firmness rather than conciliation was likely to secure peace; but that if it failed to do so "Russia should be ready to make the sacrifices required of her." The Council resolved that Vienna should be asked to extend her time limit; that Belgrade be urged "to show a desire for conciliation and to fulfil the Austrian Government's requirements in so far as they did not jeopardize the independence of the Serbian state," and that the defence ministers should request Imperial permission for the mobilisation, if events should require it, of the Odessa, Kiev, Kazan and Moscow Military Districts. Nicholas II accepted the Council's policy and himself chaired an extraordinary session on the morning of 25 July which confirmed the previous day's decisions. . . .

As a result of the decisions of the Council of Ministers on 24 and 25 July the Russian armed forces began preparations for war. On 26 July the law of 17 February/2 March 1913 on the Period Preparatory to War came into force. Magazines and supply depots were to be made ready, railway . . . personnel were to be brought up to full complement for mobilisation. . . . On the evening of 25 July at a conference of officers of the General Staff Yanushkevich called for energetic fulfilment of their tasks, stating that if necessary it was permissible slightly to overstep the strict limitations of the law in preparing the army for war. Meanwhile, as we have seen, it had been decided in principle to mobilise four military districts, Sazonov initially intending to do this should Austria invade Serbia. As later became clear, the military leaders had, however, led the Council of Ministers into error, since they failed to bring to the government's attention the difficulties that any partial mobilisation would put in the way of a subsequent general mobilisation. . . .

The results of the generals' error were not, however, immediately apparent. On 26 and 27 July Sazonov became more optimistic about the chances of avoiding war. . . . Although part of the explanation for this lies in Sazonov's unstable temperament, other factors also played a role. Like Grey, Sazonov believed the Austrian assurances that a Serb rejection of the ultimatum would not at once lead to military operations "makes the immediate situation rather less acute." . . . The events of 28 and 29 July were to disillusion the Russian Foreign Minister completely. Like Europe's other leaders he found the Serbian reply to Vienna's ultimatum astonishingly conciliatory and Austria's brusque declaration of war therefore all the more appalling. The bombardment of Belgrade convinced him that Vienna was fully committed to the immediate invasion and destruction of Serbia, while Berlin's failure to stop Austria's headlong rush into war made the Russian Foreign Ministry believe that Germany had either lost all control over its ally or, much more likely, was in spite of its assurances conniving at Austria's actions and doing nothing to check them. The final blow came on the afternoon of 29 July when Pourtalès delivered Berlin's warning that unless Russia ceased her military preparations these would lead to German mobilisation and to war. Already on 28 July Sazonov had secured Nicholas II's agreement to partial Russian mobilisation in response to Vienna's declaration of war on Serbia. The events of 29 July convinced him that war with the Central Powers was inevitable and that the vital point was to prepare to wage it with the greatest possible chance of success. He joined with the military leaders in successfully pressing general mobilisation on Nicholas II, only to see the Emperor rescind his decree and revert to partial mobilisation late in the evening of 29 July in response to a telegram from William II. On 29 and 30 July Sazonov and Yanushkevich, backed by Krivoshein, urged general mobilisation on Nicholas II on the grounds that the Central Powers were bent on war and that if

Russia delayed or, still worse, threw her plans into disarray through partial mobilisation, she would lose the war before it had ever begun. On the other side Goremykin, with the backing of at least one other minister and some of the military courtiers, urged the monarch to stick to partial mobilisation in order not to precipitate a Russo-German conflict and thus to gain time for diplomacy to find a peaceful solution. The Council of Ministers was not recalled; everything depended on Nicholas II's judgement and the impression made on him by individual advisers. Finally, on the afternoon of 30 July Sazonov persuaded the Emperor of the need for general mobilisation. German countermeasures were immediate and in Germany, unlike Russia, military planning ensured that mobilisation led automatically to war. Russia's armies could remain mobilised but behind their frontiers almost indefinitely; Germany planned for military operations almost from the first day of mobilisation in order to avert the risk of a two-front war by destroying France at the outset of the conflict. Almost precisely two days after Nicholas II's final decision for general mobilisation Pourtalès informed Sazonov that the two empires were at war.

To what extent can the Russian government be faulted for its handling of the July Crisis? Russia's key decision was the one taken on 24/25 July to support Serbian independence even at the risk of war. Given Austrian determination to crush Serbia and German willingness to back Vienna even if war with Russia and France should ensue, Petersburg's stand made a European conflict probable. Yet it is not easy to see how Russia could have acted differently in July 1914. Even leaving aside the moral, psychological, ideological and political factors which played a role here, capitulation to open Austro-German coercion would have dealt a tremendous blow to Russia's prestige and thus to her ability to defend her interests and retain her clients and allies in the Near East. . . .

Even if the Russians had pushed Belgrade into accepting every clause of the Austrian ultimatum in July 1914, it is, moreover, by no means clear that war could have been avoided save in the short run. In the weeks and months that followed capitulation to Vienna the Serbian government would probably have tried to wriggle out of the consequences of its actions. By 1914, however, Austria was unwilling to tolerate such behaviour, believing that after the events of 1906–13 only Serbia's humiliation and reduction to the status of a semi-protectorate could give Vienna a chance of checking Serb nationalism and breaking the increasing hold of Belgrade on the sympathies of the Serb and even to some extent Croat population of the Monarchy. . . .

Once Russia had decided to back Serbia the only means for the Triple Entente to avoid war lay in speedy action in London and patience in Petersburg. The British had immediately to make it clear in Berlin that should the Austro-Serb crisis develop into a European war the United Kingdom would fight on the side of Russia and France. Meanwhile, the Russians had to avoid military preparations which would precipitate armed conflict before London's message had time to be absorbed in Berlin and could result in German pressure for moderation in Vienna. . . .

How important was the general mobilisation of the Russian army on 31 July? At first glance it would seem to have been crucial since Russia's move was answered immediately by Germany's mobilisation and within two days by the outbreak of war. Even without the Russian mobilisation there is, however, every reason to doubt whether by 30 July a European conflict could have been avoided since, as Russian diplomats stressed, by then Austria and Germany had gone too far to retreat without serious damage to their prestige and to the stability of their alliance. By the time awareness of the likelihood of British intervention had caused Berlin to urge its first counsels of restraint in Vienna the Austrians were only prepared even to listen to London's calls for compromise if Russian mobilisation ceased and their offensive into Serbia was allowed to continue. Bethmann-Hollweg's half-hearted calls for moderation were in any event being undermined by Moltke's bellicose advice to Conrad. Moreover, even before he heard the news of general Russian mobilisation the German Chancellor was intending to send Petersburg a further virtual ultimatum demanding the cessation of Russia's military preparations and, as Albertini rightly states, the inevitable rejection of this demand was almost bound to lead to war. Study of the July Crisis from the Russian standpoint indeed confirms the now generally accepted view that the major immediate responsibility for the outbreak of the war rested unequivocally on the German government.

Zara Steiner

The Liberals Muddle Through to War

Zara Steiner of New Hall, Cambridge University, has published widely
on the British Foreign Office in the early part of the twentieth century.
In this selection, she traces the tortuous path that led the government
of Prime Minister Herbert Asquith and Foreign Secretary Sir Edward
Grey from indecision to continental commitment. She paints her portrait against the background of domestic unrest over Ulster, labor, and
the suffragettes, as well as the moral issue of Belgian neutrality.

"The spring and summer of 1914 were marked in Europe by an
exceptional tranquillity," Winston Churchill recalled in *The World
Crisis*. Even the arch-pessimist, Arthur Nicolson, admitted that
"Since I have been at the Foreign Office, I have not seen such calm
waters." . . . In the front quad of Balliol, undergraduates laughed
when Louis Namier warned of the prospect of a European war. At
Eton, "all seemed gaiety, sunshine and good food." Apart from
Ulster, 1914 was a fine summer. . . .

Viewed from London, the July crisis falls into two unequal parts.
Throughout the weeks of July, Grey concentrated on bringing about
a diplomatic solution of the Serbian crisis. For the most part, he
worked alone without heeding the advice of his permanent officials
or giving undue consideration to the varying opinions held by the
Cabinet or party. When it appeared to the Foreign Secretary that
war was inevitable, the battle for intervention shifted to the Cabinet.
Grey had always believed that the country would have to defend
France in a Franco-German conflict; he now had to convince those
who had never really accepted this conclusion. . . .

Almost from the start, Grey realised the gravity of the new crisis. . . . Grey's strategy was clear. In the event of a fresh crisis in the Balkans the British would work with the German government "as far as might be possible" without moving away from France and Russia. This was the policy Grey followed throughout the early weeks of the Sarajevo drama. . . .

On 24 July the Foreign Office was given the text of the ultimatum delivered at Belgrade the day before. Grey found it "the most formidable document I have ever seen addressed by one State to another that was independent." The Foreign Office was now up in arms. . . . At the close of the discussions on Ulster on the afternoon of 24 July, Grey brought up the Serbian crisis. . . . This was the first time for a month that the Cabinet discussed foreign policy. Grey suggested that the four less interested powers intervene in case of dangerous tension between Russia and Austria. . . . At a full meeting of the Cabinet on the 27th, Grey raised the issue of participation in a form which he thought would bring him the widest range of support. Would the government enter a war if France were attacked by Germany? . . . The question of Belgian neutrality would be considered at the next cabinet meeting. . . . On the 29th, "It was decided not to decide." . . .

On the question of Belgian neutrality, the Cabinet, like Gladstone's in 1870, decided that the obligation to uphold the 1839 Treaty fell on all the signatory powers collectively but not on any single one individually. If the matter arose, the decision would be "one of policy rather than legal obligations." Despite the Cabinet's caution, Grey gave [German Ambassador] Lichnowsky a private warning that if Germany and France went to war, Britain could not "stand aside and wait for any length of time." . . .

It has been argued that a blunt statement to Germany on 26 July that Britain would intervene on the side of France would have deterred the Chancellor from pushing Austria into her Serbian war. . . . Grey . . . seems not to have understood the full significance of Russian mobilisation and did not anticipate the immediate German reaction on the 31st. . . . The speed of the crisis and the rapid resort to arms threw the British off balance. But Grey had followed the wrong course during July. He had hoped until the very end that by not coming down on either side, he would delay the adoption of extreme measures. He felt personally deceived, "outraged at the way Germany and Austria have played with the most vital interests of civilization, have put aside all attempts at accommodation made by myself and others, and while continuing to negotiate have marched steadily to war." . . .

One is struck by the singular independence of the Foreign Secretary. The Foreign Office as a department was totally impotent. All who could stayed in London that final fateful weekend wanting to help but did not know how. Contemporary accounts record the sense of frustration and despair with which the senior officials watched the course of events. . . . There was no confidential private secretary to record Grey's inner thoughts but the sense of singular responsibility pervades his autobiography written eleven years later. . . .

Grey remained, as he had always been, curiously obtuse about the military and naval ties between Britain and France. . . . The top army echelon believed that they were ready for a European war. "What a real piece of luck this war has been as regards Ireland — just averted a Civil War and when it is over we may all be tired of fighting," Sir William Birdwood remarked a few months after war broke out. . . . The navy was more fortunate in its civilian leadership. Churchill acted on his own initiative. On 29 July, the Cabinet agreed to the First Lord's request for a precautionary mobilisation of the fleet. . . .

The Prime Minister wrote to Miss Stanley on 2 August: "I suppose a good 3/4 of our own party in the House of Commons are for absolute non-interference at any price." . . . Most of the population had barely heard of Serbia and certainly did not know where it was. Yet by the 3rd, ministers sensed that the war would be popular. . . . Belgium proved to be a catalyst which unleashed the many emotions, rationalisations and glorifications of war which had long been part of the British climate of opinion. Having a moral cause, all the latent anti-German feeling, fed by years of naval rivalry and assumed enmity, rose to the surface. The "scrap of paper" proved decisive both in maintaining the unity of the government and then in providing a focal point for public feeling. . . .

Events moved rapidly; ministers felt that they were living in a world created by H. G. Wells. But the Cabinet's hesitations arose less from a sense of helplessness than from an understandable unwillingness to face the ultimate question. Confusion and lack of leadership prevented the emergence of an anti-war party; the rapid plunge into actual war, amazingly fast by contemporary standards, made rational thought difficult. . . . The issue of Belgium was all-important because the radical conscience needed a *raison d'être*. Their followers could not be told that Britain had entered the war to uphold the balance of power. A German attack on France involved British interests. The Cabinet had resisted this conclusion for many years; ministers now cloaked their final choice in moral terms. . . .

In August 1914 the Cabinet was free to make the ultimate choice between peace and war. Having put only one foot into Europe in the years which preceded the Sarajevo crisis, it had become necessary to find a reason for taking the ultimate step which would check a German bid for mastery in Europe. The German invasion of Belgium provided the answer to a dilemma which the Liberals themselves had created. But even in August, they did not wish to pay the full price and until the very end shrank from accepting the bill. A naval war would be an honourable but inexpensive way to safeguard British interests. Grey . . . hoped by his half-committed policies to avoid the final Armageddon. . . . He never spelt out the reasons for a continental commitment, or its possible costs. . . .

Even as the ministers drove to the Commons to hear Grey speak, they knew that the public would support their decision. Holiday crowds, influenced perhaps by their sheer numbers and close proximity to the centre of events, cheered lustily. . . .

On the 5th, Asquith summoned a War Council in which the generals debated where the troops should be sent and how many divisions should go. Henry Wilson explained that all was arranged for landings in France; Sir John French, the designated commander of the B.E.F., preferred Antwerp. Grey and Churchill supported Wilson. Kitchener, the Secretary of State for War, suggested, in view of the late intervention, that Amiens rather than Mauberge [*sic*] be used as a staging area. After "some desultory strategy (some thinking Liège was in Holland) and idiocy," the Council accepted Lord Roberts's advice to let the French decide. . . .

"I hate war! I hate war!" Grey was torn between his belief that the war would be a short one and his deep-seated fear that it would prove a terrible catastrophe.

Georges Clemenceau and Woodrow Wilson leave Versailles Palace on 28 June 1919, having reordered the world. (The Granger Collection)

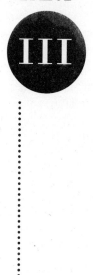

The Question of War Guilt

Commission on War Guilt (1919)

The Charge: German War Guilt

The Commission on the Responsibility of the Authors of the War and on Enforcement of Penalties was created at the plenary session of the Paris Peace Conference on January 25, 1919. Two representatives of each of the five great powers (France, Great Britain, Italy, Japan, and the United States) and one each from Belgium, Greece, Poland, Rumania, and Serbia made up its membership; U.S. Secretary of State Robert Lansing was chosen chairman of the commission. The report, concluded toward the end of March, was unanimously adopted at the conference on May 6, 1919. The first chapter, reprinted below, is based largely upon

From the *German White Book Concerning the Responsibility of the Authors of the War* (New York, 1924), pp. 15–21. Used with the permission of the Carnegie Endowment for International Peace.

documents, often carefully edited, issued by the belligerents in the various "colored books" shortly after the outbreak of the war.

On the question of the responsibility of the authors of the war, the Commission, after having examined a number of official documents relating to the origin of the World War, and to the violations of neutrality and of frontiers which accompanied its inception, has determined that the responsibility for it lies wholly upon the Powers which declared war in pursuance of a policy of aggression, the concealment of which gives to the origin of this war the character of a dark conspiracy against the peace of Europe.

This responsibility rests first on Germany and Austria, secondly on Turkey and Bulgaria. The responsibility is made all the graver by reason of the violation by Germany and Austria of the neutrality of Belgium and Luxemburg, which they themselves had guaranteed. It is increased, with regard to both France and Serbia, by the violation of their frontiers before the declaration of war.

Premeditation of the War: Germany and Austria

Many months before the crisis of 1914 the German Emperor had ceased to pose as the champion of peace. Naturally believing in the overwhelming superiority of his Army, he openly showed his enmity towards France. General von Moltke said to the King of the Belgians: "This time the matter must be settled." In vain the King protested. The Emperor and his Chief of Staff remained no less fixed in their attitude.

On the 28th of June, 1914, occurred the assassination at Sarajevo of the heir-apparent of Austria. "It is the act of a little group of madmen," said Francis Joseph. The act, committed as it was by a subject of Austria-Hungary on Austro-Hungarian territory, could in no way compromise Serbia, which very correctly expressed its condolences and stopped public rejoicings in Belgrade. If the Government of Vienna thought that there were any Serbian complicity, Serbia was ready to seek out the guilty parties. But this attitude failed to satisfy Austria and still less Germany, who, after their first astonishment had passed, saw in this royal and national misfortune a pretext to initiate war.

At Potsdam a "decisive consultation" took place on the 5th of July, 1914. Vienna and Berlin decided upon this plan: "Vienna will send to Belgrade a very emphatic ultimatum with a very short limit of time."

The Bavarian Minister, von Lerchenfeld, said in a confidential dispatch dated the 18th of July, 1914, the facts stated in which have never been officially denied: "It is clear that Serbia cannot accept the demands, which are inconsistent with the dignity of an independent state." Count Lerchenfeld reveals in this report that, at the time it was made, the ultimatum to Serbia had been jointly decided upon by the Governments of Berlin and Vienna; that they were waiting to send it until President Poincaré and Mr. Viviani should have left for St. Petersburg; and that no illusions were cherished, either at Berlin or Vienna, as to the consequences which this threatening measure would involve. It was perfectly well known that war would be the result.

The Bavarian Minister explains, moreover, that the only fear of the Berlin Government was that Austria-Hungary might hesitate and draw back at the last minute, and that on the other hand Serbia, on the advice of France and Great Britain, might yield to the pressure put upon her. Now, "the Berlin Government considers that war is necessary." Therefore, it gave full powers to Count Berchtold, who instructed the Ballplatz on the 18th of July, 1914, to negotiate with Bulgaria to induce her to enter into an alliance and to participate in the war.

In order to mask this understanding, it was arranged that the Emperor should go for a cruise in the North Sea, and that the Prussian Minister of War should go for a holiday, so that the Imperial Government might pretend that events had taken it completely by surprise.

Austria suddenly sent Serbia an ultimatum that she had carefully prepared in such a way as to make it impossible to accept. Nobody could be deceived; "the whole world understands that this ultimatum means war." According to Mr. Sazonoff [Sazanov], "Austria-Hungary wanted to devour Serbia."

Mr. Sazonoff asked Vienna for an extension of the short time-limit of forty-eight hours given by Austria to Serbia for the most serious decision in its history. Vienna refused the demand. On the 24th and 25th of July, England and France multiplied their efforts to persuade Serbia to satisfy the Austro-Hungarian demands. Russia threw in her weight on the side of conciliation.

Contrary to the expectation of Austria-Hungary and Germany, Serbia yielded. She agreed to all the requirements of the ultimatum, subject to the single reservation that, in the judicial inquiry which she would commence for the purpose of seeking out the guilty parties, the participation of Austrian officials would be kept within the limits assigned by international law. "If the Austro-Hungarian Government is not satisfied with this," Serbia declared she was ready "to submit to the decision of the Hague Tribunal."

"A quarter of an hour before the expiration of the time limit," at 5:45 on the 25th, Mr. Pashitch [Pašić], the Serbian Minister for Foreign Affairs, delivered his reply to Baron Giesl, the Austro-Hungarian Minister.

On Mr. Pashitch's return to his own office he found awaiting him a letter from Baron Giesl saying that he was not satisfied with the reply. At 6:30 the latter had left Belgrade, and even before he had arrived at Vienna, the Austro-Hungarian Government had handed his passports to Mr. Yovanovitch, the Serbian Minister, and had prepared thirty-three mobilization proclamations, which were published on the following morning in the *Budapesti Kozlöni*, the official gazette of the Hungarian Government. On the 27th Sir Maurice de Bunsen telegraphed to Sir Edward Grey: "this country has gone wild with joy at the prospect of war with Serbia." At midday on the 28th Austria declared war on Serbia. On the 29th the Austrian army commenced the bombardment of Belgrade, and made its dispositions to cross the frontier.

The reiterated suggestions of the Entente Powers with a view to finding a peaceful solution of the dispute only produced evasive replies on the part of Berlin or promises of intervention with the Government of Vienna without any effectual steps being taken.

On the 24th of July Russia and England asked that the Powers should be granted a reasonable delay in which to work in concert for the maintenance of peace. Germany did not join in this request.

On the 25th of July Sir Edward Grey proposed mediation by four Powers (England, France, Italy and Germany). France and Italy immediately gave their concurrence. Germany refused, alleging that it was not a question of mediation but of arbitration, as the conference of the four Powers was called to make proposals, not to decide.

On the 26th of July Russia proposed to negotiate directly with Austria. Austria refused.

On the 27th of July England proposed a European conference. Germany refused.

On the 29th of July Sir Edward Grey asked the Wilhelmstrasse to be good enough to "suggest any method by which the influence of the four Powers could be used together to prevent a war between Austria and Russia." She was asked to say what she desired. Her reply was evasive.

On the same day, the 29th of July, the Czar dispatched to the Emperor William II a telegram suggesting that the Austro-Serbian problem should be submitted to the Hague Tribunal. The suggestion received no reply. This important telegram does not appear in the German White Book. It was made public by the Petrograd *Official Gazette* (January, 1915).

The Bavarian Legation, in a report dated the 31st of July, declared its conviction that the efforts of Sir Edward Grey to preserve peace would not hinder the march of events.

As early as the 21st of July German mobilization had commenced by the recall of a certain number of classes of the reserve, then of German officers in Switzerland, and finally of the Metz garrison on the 25th of July. On the 26th of July the German fleet was called back from Norway.

The Entente did not relax its conciliatory efforts, but the German Government systematically brought all its attempts to nought. When Austria consented for the first time on the 31st of July to discuss the contents of the Serbian note with the Russian Government and the Austro-Hungarian Ambassador received orders to "converse" with the Russian Minister of Foreign Affairs, Germany made any negotiations impossible by sending her ultimatum to Russia. Prince Lichnowsky wrote that "a hint from Berlin would have been enough to decide Count Berchtold to content himself with a diplomatic success and to declare that he was satisfied with the Serbian reply, but this hint was not given. *On the contrary they went forward towards war.*"

On the 1st of August the German Emperor addressed a telegram to the King of England containing the following sentence: "The troops on my frontier are, at this moment, being kept back by telegraphic and telephonic orders from crossing the French frontier." Now, war was not declared till two days after that date, and as the German mobilization orders were issued on that same day, the 1st of August, it follows that, as a matter of fact, the German Army had been mobilized and concentrated in pursuance of previous orders.

The attitude of the Entente nevertheless remained still to the very end so conciliatory that, at the very time at which the German fleet was bombarding Libau, Nicholas II gave his word of honor to William II that Russia would not undertake any aggressive action during the *pourparlers*, and that when the German troops commenced their march across the French frontier Mr. Viviani telegraphed to all the French Ambassadors "we must not stop working for accommodation."

On the 3rd of August Mr. von Schoen went to the Quai d'Orsay with the declaration of war against France. Lacking a real cause of complaint, Germany alleged, in her declaration of war, that bombs had been dropped by French airplanes in various districts in Germany. This statement was entirely false. Moreover, it was either later admitted to be so or no particulars were ever furnished by the German Government.

Moreover, in order to be manifestly above reproach, France was careful to withdraw her troops ten kilometers from the German frontier. Notwithstanding this precaution, numerous officially established violations of French territory preceded the declaration of war.

The provocation was so flagrant that Italy, herself a member of the Triple Alliance, did not hesitate to declare that in view of the aggressive character of the war the *casus foederis* ceased to apply.

Conclusions

1. The war was premeditated by the Central Powers together with their Allies, Turkey and Bulgaria, and was the result of acts deliberately committed in order to make it unavoidable.
2. Germany, in agreement with Austria-Hungary, deliberately worked to defeat all the many conciliatory proposals made by the Entente Powers and their repeated efforts to avoid war.

John Röhl

1914: Delusion or Design?

John Röhl of the University of Sussex, England, is best known for his work, *Germany After Bismarck*, and as editor of three volumes of the political correspondence of Kaiser Wilhelm II's friend Philipp Eulenburg. He has just published the first volume of a biography of the kaiser and is the foremost expert on Wilhelm II. In this selection, partly based on Eulenburg's papers, Röhl argues that Germany was determined to unleash war in Europe, possibly as early as 1912 and definitely in 1914.

The controversy over the immediate causes of the First World War appears at last to be drawing to a close. After the works of Luigi Albertini, Fritz Fischer and Imanuel Geiss, scholars the world over are agreed that the major responsibility for this previously unparalleled catastrophe must be sought in Berlin. . . . Fischer's originally so controversial views are now "more or less generally accepted by West German historians." What is still in dispute, however, even after the appearance of Fischer's latest book *Krieg der Illusionen*, are the motives behind Germany's fateful policy in the crisis. . . . Were the statesmen of the Central Powers "merely" pursuing a policy of "calculated risk" with the intention of tilting the balance of power in their favour, if possible without a major war, and would they have undertaken this "leap into the dark" if they had assessed the consequences of their action — and particularly Britain's participation in the war — more accurately? Was it a "preventive war," and if so, was the threat it was designed to pre-empt real, or only imagined? Or was this a war of aggression with the aim of securing German domination

From *1914: Delusion or Design? The testimony of two German diplomats*, pp. 21–36, ed. John Röhl. Published by Elek, London. Copyright 1973 by John Röhl.

over the European continent while there was still time? Was the war planned, or the result of a terrible miscalculation?

The degree to which German policy in 1914 was the product of "design" or "delusion" is a question which will surely occupy historians for many years to come, for the final answer will hardly be a simple one. A major difficulty is that the terms in which the discussion has hitherto been conducted — "calculated risk," "preventive war," and "war of conquest" — are all revealed in the light of the latest available evidence to be oversimplifications. The "calculated risk" theory holds that it was Germany's intention not to go to war but merely to use the threat of a major war to force Russia to break with her allies, France and Britain, and join the German bloc instead. This theory, which has been ingeniously distilled from the public writings of Chancellor Bethmann Hollweg's confidant Kurt Riezler, does indeed receive an element of support from the latter's private diaries which . . . provide one of the best insights we are ever likely to get into Bethmann's real aims in 1914. . . .

Whatever his personal preference, however, it is certain that Bethmann from the outset assessed the chances of Germany's emerging from the crisis without a war as very slender indeed. And yet he persisted in his disastrous policy to the bitter end, in spite of the several opportunities he had of pulling back from the brink without loss of face. . . . The term "calculated risk" seems singularly inappropriate to describe such reckless behavior: the title of one of Riezler's books, *Die Erforderlichkeiten des Unmöglichen* — "the need for the impossible" — would seem to supply a more apposite description. We must conclude that German policy in July 1914 was either not calculated at all, or that it was calculated to produce a war.

The concept of "preventive war" is no less problematical than the "calculated risk" theory. In its narrowest sense, a preventive war is one in which a state facing the undoubted threat of immediate aggression by a hostile power or coalition of powers decides that attack is the best means of defence and takes the offensive. . . . It is known that one of Bethmann Hollweg's chief preoccupations in the July crisis was to make Russia appear as the aggressor so as to persuade the German nation that it must defend itself. "The mood is brilliant," the head of the Kaiser's Navy Cabinet could write on 1 August 1914. "The government has succeeded very well in making us appear as the attacked."

In the case of German policy in 1914, however, an even greater difficulty arises. No serious historian now claims that the Triple Entente actually planned to attack Germany. On the other hand there is a great deal of evidence which indicates that German generals in 1914 and earlier were obsessed with the idea that by about 1916 Russia would be "ready," and that Germany, if she were going to have a chance of winning, had better strike now rather than later. In this peculiarly German sense, and this sense alone, can the German government be said to have taken "preventive" action in 1914. But to apply the adjective "preventive" to a war begun because of vague pessimistic prognostications of this sort, however deeply they may have been felt, is to depart a long way from the original meaning of that term. Indeed, it is then hard to distinguish between a preventive war and a war of aggression.

Moreover, that distinction becomes doubly difficult to draw if we accept the view of Fritz Fischer . . . that the German decision to fight a major war was taken not in July 1914 in response to the Sarajevo murders or any other immediate threat, but a year and a half earlier, on 8 December 1912! We now possess no less than three independent records of the remarkable "war council" (the description is Bethmann Hollweg's) summoned by the Kaiser that Sunday morning. At this conference of Army and Navy leaders — the "civilian" statesmen were not even invited — the Kaiser anticipated with breath-taking accuracy the exact sequence of events of July 1914. Wilhelm II was in a fit of anger over reports from his new ambassador in London, Prince Lichnowsky, about a conversation with the British War Minister Lord Haldane in which the latter had warned that "England could not tolerate Germany's becoming the dominant Power on the Continent and uniting it under her leadership," and would therefore always side with France in a European war. The Kaiser opened the conference by describing Haldane's statement as "a desirable clarification of the situation for the benefit of those who had felt sure of England." As there was now no further reason for further restraint he recommended strong action by Austria against Serbia in the Balkan War which had just begun, even though he realised that "if Russia supports the Serbs, as she evidently does . . . then war would be unavoidable for us too." This prospect did not unduly concern him, however, for Austria would probably find allies in Bulgaria, Rumania, Albania and Turkey, and "if these Powers join

Austria then we shall be free to fight the war with full fury [*mit voller Wucht*] against France." The Fleet, the Kaiser said, "must naturally prepare itself for the war against England." There would have to be "immediate submarine warfare against English troop transports in the Scheldt or by Dunkirk [and] mine warfare in the Thames." The Chief of the General Staff, Moltke, "wanted to launch an immediate attack." In his view, "war was unavoidable, and the sooner the better." There had, Moltke said, "not been a more favourable opportunity since the formation of the Triple Alliance." Tirpitz on the other hand demanded a "postponement of the great fight for one and a half years" (two of the sources say "for one year") "until the [Kiel] Canal and the U-Boat harbour on Heligoland were finished." Wilhelm, one of the reports continues, "agreed to a postponement only reluctantly." This delay was, however, to be put to good use: the press was to be used "to prepare the popularity of a war against Russia." . . . On the day after the council, the Kaiser informed the Archduke Franz Ferdinand of Austria that Haldane's statement had been "typically English!" that is, "full of poison and hatred and envy of the good development of our alliance and our two countries! It did not surprise me, and the necessary preparations are being made."

The interpretation of these newly discovered documents on the "war council" of December 1912 is now central to the entire controversy on the origins of the War. . . . At least the "war council" itself must be regarded as one of the most obvious signs that the Army had regained its traditional position of pre-eminence in Prussia-Germany after the collapse of Tirpitz's originally grandiose naval plans and the fiasco of the Agadir crisis of 1911. And it is now hardly disputed that the Army was pressing for war, and did so the more persistently the more its influence within the German power-structure grew. It is a curious fact that, only a few weeks after the conference of 8 December 1912, the German General Staff tore up the only plan it had which envisaged an initial offensive on the eastern front. Was this not . . . a sign that a firm decision to implement the Schlieffen Plan (for a lightning war against first France and then Russia) had already been taken? One very clear instance of Army pressure is the "almost ultimative" demand for a so-called preventive war made by General von Moltke in late May or early June 1914. Gottlieb von Jagow, the German Foreign Secretary, recalled that on a journey from Potsdam to Berlin,

Moltke described to me his opinion of our military situation. The prospects of the future oppressed him heavily. In two to three years Russia would have completed her armaments. The military superiority of our enemies would then be so great that he did not know how he could overcome them. Today we would still be a match for them. In his opinion there was no alternative to making preventive war in order to defeat the enemy while we still had a chance of victory. The Chief of the General Staff therefore proposed that I should conduct a policy with the aim of provoking a war in the near future.

Finally, the most obvious point must not be overlooked: at the council of 8 December 1912, Tirpitz was apparently cornered by the "war party" and forced, in the Kaiser's presence, into giving not only a date when a war could be started, but also a plausible justification for delaying the war till then. He gave as his reason the need to complete the U-Boat harbour on Heligoland and the widening of the Kiel Canal, so that dreadnoughts could pass (admittedly as yet only unladen) from the Baltic to the North Sea. The widened Kiel Canal was ceremoniously opened on 24 June 1914, four days before Sarajevo; the first ship-of-the-line passed through it one month later, on 25 July! Was this really just coincidence? If not, if the First World War was in some sense "planned" and prepared well in advance, then the "preventive" element in the German decision becomes so hazy as to amount to little more than the feeling that it would be easier to "impose one's will on the enemy" (Clausewitz) sooner rather than later.

The third and final position we must briefly examine is the thesis that the First World War was a war of aggression and of conquest by Germany. Perhaps such terms seem inappropriate because of their association with Hitler and the Nuremberg trials, but then Fritz Fischer . . . has documented the very close similarity, at least in geographical extent, between the German aims in the two world wars. . . . It was Fischer's discovery and publication of Bethmann Hollweg's "September Programme" which, once the storm caused by his book had blown over, necessitated a complete revision of the accepted interpretation of the First World War and the course of modern German history in general. On 9 September 1914, only five weeks after the outbreak of war and after consultation with leading figures in government and industrial circles, the Reich Chancellor drew up plans to establish German control over almost the entire

continent of Europe "for all imaginable time." . . . Bethmann Hollweg's memorandum was not, admittedly, a "binding" government
programme. But the war aims it listed have now been shown to be
paradigmatic of German aspirations before and during the War. . . .

Our examination of the three basic explanations for Germany's
policy in June 1914 has shown them to have a great deal more in
common with one another than might at first be supposed. None of
the leaders in Berlin believed the chances of Germany's emerging
from the crisis without a major war to be more than minimal; on the
contrary, a policy was adopted even by the "moderates" in the full
knowledge that a European war would be the most probable result.
None of the Berlin leaders believed that Germany was in immediate
danger of being attacked; if they talked nevertheless of the need for a
"preventive war," it was in the very loose sense that if Germany were
to make her "bid for world power," she had better act before Austria
became too weak, and the Entente Powers too strong to stop her. On
the other hand the subjective mood of the men who took the "leap
into the dark" in 1914 was far removed from the carefree optimism
that one might have expected in so powerful and dynamic a nation;
rather, it was an incongruous compound of optimism and pessimism
which is perhaps best summed up in that popular German catch-
word of the time: *Weltmacht oder Niedergang*, world power or down-
fall. Though there is undoubtedly a lot of work still to be done to
analyse which groups within the far from monolithic German government — the Court, the Army, the Navy, the Chancellor and the
Foreign Office to list just the most obvious of them — advocated
which course of action at what point in time and for what reasons,
one thing seems beyond dispute: the First World War was no acci-
dent for which all the belligerents bore an equal share of the responsibility, but was to a greater or lesser extent "willed" by the German
Reich.

Imanuel Geiss

The Fischer "Controversy" and German War Guilt

Imanuel Geiss, professor of history at Bremen University, offers his view of German reactions to Fischer's controversial interpretation of the origins of the First World War. Moreover, he restates his own convictions, based on his two-volume edition of documents pertaining to the July Crisis of 1914, concerning the degree of Austrian, German, and Entente responsibility for the war.

Fischer not only questioned the taboo built up over five decades by successive political regimes in Germany; he also broke the monopoly of knowledge held by conservative or mildly conservative-liberal historians, in a historical problem which may well rank as one of the most complicated and bewildering in modern history. He did it just by picking up Albertini and reading the documents published since 1919.

The leading German historians rushed angrily into print to denounce Fischer and closed ranks against the heretic. . . . Erwin Hölzle from the right joined forces with Golo Mann, Ludwig Dehio, and Hans Herzfeld of the "left," while Gerhard Ritter from his centre position turned out to be Fischer's most persistent critic. . . . After the initial formation of a united front against Fischer, three major groups emerged. One, led by Hans Rothfels, stuck to their traditional guns and said there was nothing to revise. A second, headed by Gerhard Ritter and Michael Freund, though criticizing the older German literature on July 1914 as "too apologetic" (Ritter) or even denouncing the traditional line as the "Unschuldslüge" [non-war-guilt lie] (Freund), still maintained most of their old arguments.

From Imanuel Geiss, "The Outbreak of the First World War and German War Aims," *The Journal of Contemporary History*, vol. 1 (July 1966), pp. 75–91. Reprinted with permission.

A third group, represented by Egmont Zechlin and Karl-Dietrich Erdmann, have at least in part abandoned the old positions, although very discreetly and without giving any credit to Fischer. They now admit that Germany in July 1914 deliberately risked war, even with Britain, but they hedge this vital admission with a number of "explanations" which only tend to obscure the central issue. Zechlin argues that Bethmann Hollweg, when taking the plunge in July 1914, only wanted a limited, "rational" war in eighteenth-century style, not a ferocious world war. . . . Erdmann gives a psychological portrait of the Chancellor, based mainly on the diary of Kurt Riezler, Bethmann Hollweg's close adviser, and stresses the Chancellor's subjective honesty, his rejection of world domination for Germany. . . .

Another myth also had to go for good — the myth of *Einkreisung.* There was no "encirclement" of Germany by enemies waiting to attack and crush her. The partition of Europe and the world into two power blocks, with the Triple Entente on the one hand, the Triple Alliance on the other, was largely a result of German policy, of the German desire to raise the Reich from the status of a continental power to that of a world power. . . . It was only after Germany started on her ambitious and ill-fated career of becoming a full-fledged world power in her own right that the world situation changed radically. Britain, challenged by Germany's naval programme more than by her territorial claims, notably in Africa, abandoned her "splendid isolation" and sought alliances, first with Japan in 1902, then with France in 1904, and finally, in 1907, with Russia. What was — and to a certain extent still is — denounced in Germany as *Einkreisung,* amounted to the containment of German ambitions which ran counter to the interests of all other imperialist powers.

The concept of encirclement, however, played an important part immediately before the outbreak of war in 1914. In Germany the idea had become widespread that the only choice for the Reich was between rising to a full-fledged world power and stagnation. The German *Weltanschauung* saw only the unending struggle of all against all; this social-Darwinistic concept was not limited to the lunatic fringe, but influenced even the most liberal spokesman of the Wilhelmian establishment, Riezler, Bethmann Hollweg's young protégé. For him all nations had the desire for permanent expansion with world domination as the supreme goal. Since he looked upon any containment of German aspirations as a hostile act, Riezler's ideas, translated into official policy, were bound to make war unavoidable. . . .

The final logical conclusion was the idea of preventive war against those enemies who tried to block Germany's further rise. The traditional school in Germany always indignantly denied the existence of the preventive war concept even among the Prussian General Staff. The prevailing spirit of militarism and social-Darwinism in Wilhelmian Germany made it, however, more than plausible. . . . In February 1918 ex-Chancellor Bethmann Hollweg, questioned privately by the liberal politician Conrad Haussmann, said: "Yes, My God, in a certain sense it was a preventive war. But when war was hanging above us, when it had to come in two years even more dangerously and more inescapably, and when the generals said, now it is still possible, without defeat, but not in two years time. Yes, the generals!" . . .

The German General Staff. . . was ready to welcome Sarajevo as the golden opportunity for risking a preventive war. . . . Wilhelm II was incensed at the murder, perhaps most because it attacked his cherished monarchist principle. When he received the report of Tschirschky, the German ambassador to Vienna, of 30 June, telling of his moderating counsels to the Austrians, the Kaiser commented in his usual wild manner and provided the specious slogan "Now or never!" which turned out to be the guiding star of German diplomacy in the crisis of July 1914. . . .

In trying to assess the shares of responsibility for the war two basic distinctions have to be made: on the one hand between the three stages of war connected with its outbreak: local war (Austria v. Serbia), continental war (Austria and Germany v. Russia and France), and world war (Britain joining the continental war). . . . On the other hand, one has to distinguish between the will to start any of those three stages of war and the fact of merely causing them.

Since the world war developed out of a local war, then of continental war, the major share for causing it lies with that power which willed the local and/or continental war. That power was clearly Germany. She did not will the world war, as is borne out by her hopes of keeping out Britain, but she did urge Austria to make war on Serbia. . . . Germany, furthermore, was the only power which had no objection to the continental war. So long as Britain kept out, she was confident of winning a war against Russia and France. Germany did nothing to prevent continental war, even at the risk of a world war, a risk which her government had seen from the beginning.

Austria, of course, wanted a local war . . . but feared a continental war. In fact, she hoped that Germany, by supporting her diplomatically, might frighten Russia into inaction.

Russia, France, and Britain tried to avert continental war. Their main argument for mediation between Serbia and Austria was precisely that to prevent the local war would be the best means of averting continental war. On the other hand, they contributed to the outbreak, each in her own way: Russia by committing the technical blunder of providing the cue for German mobilization, instead of waiting until Germany had mobilized. The French attitude was almost entirely correct; her only fault was that she could not hold back her Russian ally from precipitate general mobilization. Britain might have made her stand clear beyond any doubt much earlier, since this might have been a way of restraining Germany, although it is doubtful whether this would have altered the course of events to any appreciable degree. The share of the Entente powers is much smaller than Germany's, for it consisted mainly in reacting — not always in the best manner — to German action.

Looking back on the events . . . , the outbreak of the first world war looks like the original example of faulty brinkmanship, of rapid escalation in a period of history when the mechanisms of alliances and mobilization schedules could still work unchecked by fear of the absolute weapon and the absolute destruction its use would bring in what would now be the third world war.

Gerhard Ritter

Anti-Fischer: A New War-Guilt Thesis?

Gerhard Ritter, professor of history at Freiburg University from 1924 to 1956, is best known for his book *The Schlieffen Plan*, as well as for his four-volume opus, *The Sword and the Scepter: The Problem of Militarism in Germany*. A veteran of the Great War, Ritter after the Second World War was willing to reexamine and to revise modestly the conservative literature on the war-guilt controversy, but he could not accept Fischer's radical position. In fact, until his death in 1967, Ritter was Fischer's most persistent critic. He attacked Fischer for inaccuracies of interpretation and emphasis, and for failing to understand the meaning of his sources within their historical context. In the end, Ritter considered Fischer's works a "national tragedy."

It is part of Fischer's basic thesis that the German government, instead of seeking peace, actually considered war as necessary (in view of the development in the ratios of military strength) and saw in the July crisis of 1914 an especially favorable opportunity for a "great diplomatic success" which would push Russia completely out of the Balkans.

But was our goal really this rather than the maintenance of our Austrian ally as a great power? In other words, is the German policy of 1914 to be understood as aggressive or defensive? Around that question in the final analysis revolved the vast controversy of historians of all countries, which since 1919 has brought to light mountains of documentary sources and monographs and which Fischer again revives. Nothing can be more troublesome and more unpleasant than to argue with him — just when one, like myself, is convinced that the older German war-guilt literature of the twenties and thirties has proved to be all too apologetic and in need of some revision.

From Gerhard Ritter, "Eine neue Kriegsschuldthese?" *Historische Zeitschrift*, v. 194 (June 1962), pp. 657–668, translated by D. E. Lee and Stewart A. Stehlin. Reprinted with permission. Footnotes omitted.

For a problem so difficult, so over-discussed, and so over-laden with source materials as the war-guilt question requires endless patience and conscientious care in the analysis of documentary evidence. Nowhere is there less room for "thesis history" than here.

Fischer explains, moreover, that he did not want to treat the war-guilt question anew, yet in fact he has done that. Only he already knew beforehand what he had to prove and proceeded into the collections of documents without being too selective.

As the first state witness for the Berlin government he brings forward a journalist, not a diplomat, Viktor Naumann, who as early as July 1 tried to persuade the General Secretary of the Vienna foreign ministry, Count Hoyos, to press for the attack on Serbia and promised him to work in the same sense in Berlin. Naumann was only the representative of patriotic currents of opinion in Germany, but had heard in the foreign office through Councillor von Stumm that they were greatly worried there over the rapidly growing Russian armament, and he thought (apparently correctly) that it was permissible to conclude from this and similar expressions that in the foreign office "they no longer rejected quite so completely the idea of a preventive war against Russia as they had a year before." That is really all there was to the matter. But the journalist attached to this idea political considerations concerning the necessity of risking even a European war because of Serbia, for which the Dual Alliance "was now still strong enough." That was grist for Count Hoyos' mill, truly the least hesitant of all the Austrian warmongers, who then reported this conversation in detail to his minister. Fischer finds the conversation of "great significance," since Naumann's predictions were to be accurately confirmed by Germany's conduct in the July crisis. In fact they correspond accurately with the Fischer thesis. Are they, however, proof that the chancellor and the chief of the general staff wanted to unloose a preventive war?

The relation of the two allies is so portrayed by Fischer that Austrian policy was fundamentally peacefully oriented, and only through the greatest pressure by Berlin did Austria allow herself to be pushed into war. The Sarajevo assassination, so goes the account, was received in Austria with conflicting emotions, in part even with relief that the Slavophil heir to the throne had at last gone. Only a group around General Conrad had wanted to "settle accounts" with Serbia, but they were also hesitant. In contrast, from July 6, German policy, submitting without opposition to the monarchical opinions of Emperor William, pressed, not without threats concerning future alliance relations, for the strongest action even to the point of war. Now there is certainly no doubt that in Vienna they were anxious and uncertain so long as they had not made sure (through a special mission of Count Hoyos) that the German government was ready, just as in 1908 and differently than in 1912, to cover its ally in case of a conflict with Russia. From that, however, one cannot say that the initiative for the "settlement" with Serbia was forced upon the Austrians half violently by Berlin. It was they who requested support in Berlin, not vice-versa; and it means putting the course of events upside down when Fischer tries to ascribe responsibility to the German instead of the Austrian government for its disastrous diplomacy — and strategy — as lame as it was frivolous and insincere in the decisive weeks.

He obviously cannot — or will not — comprehend what the true motive was for the many Berlin admonitions advising Austria to take quick and energetic action. It was not a burning eagerness for war of some kind of militarist, but rather the very well-justified fear of the dilatory half-measures of the Austrians. . . . Granted that German policy in the July crisis relied upon false speculation. Indeed, it had falsely evaluated almost all factors: underestimated the war preparedness of Russia and France, overestimated the impression of outrage upon the courts of Europe and the peacefulness of English policy, and, not least, far overvalued the military capacity, political wisdom and manageability of the Austrian ally. One can even ask after that whether their basic assumption had not been faulty; whether the maintenance of the Danubian empire as a great power was still worth such a huge risk; yes, whether it was even possible in the long run. . . . But the historian who asks such questions will still be aware that he therewith completely departs from a historical understanding of that period. . . . For the decision of 1866 had still not divided the German nation so deeply that in imperial Germany they could look with equanimity upon the ruin of the "brother empire" (whose maintenance even Bismarck had always declared a European necessity); quite apart from the fact that at this period still they considered a Russian-dominated Balkans, including Hungary, as an unbearable threat to Central Europe. Thus, even Prince Lichnowsky, our London ambassador and the sharpest critic of the

Berlin government's policy, explained in a private letter to [Foreign Secretary] Jagow that the idea of sacrificing Austria as an ally was farthest from his mind, but he did take the view that a military "punishment" of Serbia was a thoughtless folly of Viennese policy. . . . If the monarchy, however, let the Sarajevo murder, the strongest of all provocations, pass without doing anything, then its rapid decline would no longer be delayed.

But if such a powerful stroke seemed to both governments to be necessary, then the blow must fall immediately. . . . And thus, for Berlin, it was the most terrible disappointment when little by little it turned out that the Imperial and Royal army was not in fact able to do that, not even after detailed preparations which dragged out finally until August 12 — and then denuded the Galician border of troops which thereby left Germany completely alone on the Russian front. Thus, then, the impression of almost all remarks of responsible German officials in the July weeks is that of a permanently growing and ever more severely oppressive anxiety. To overlook that and to discover some kind of desire for battle and confidence of victory is only possible with the help of radical and round-about interpretations. . . . And does Fischer seriously believe that Prime Minister Count Stürgkh's anxiety that Austria would lose Germany's support in the future through feeble hesitation "refutes" the view presented from previous research that we intervened on behalf of the Danubian monarchy in order not to sacrifice the last important ally?

Like the attitude of the German politicians, that of the leading military men is put entirely in a wrong light. Moltke is said to have spoken out in his last Karlsbad conversation with Conrad von Hötzendorf for a "speedy attack" and therefore had shown himself resolutely in favor of war. Not a word about that exists in the sources. . . . Moltke was certainly greatly distressed by the prospect of Russia surpassing us in armaments even further in the coming years . . . so that "every delay meant the lessening of the chances" — a worry which he appears to have expressed many times in the summer of 1914. Fischer has completely ignored my proof that these may not be taken as eagerness for war. He appears to find somehow as striking the harmless communication of the Quartermaster General Waldersee to Jagow that . . . the general staff was certainly "ready' (namely with its deployment plans and preparations for mobilization that were routinely drawn up anew every spring), for Fischer calls attention to the words "ready" and "prepared." On the same level is his interpretation of a letter in which Bethmann Holl-weg, on July 16, asked the State Secretary of Alsace, Count Roedern, to prevent possible Francophobe remarks by the Alsatian press; French chauvinism was not to be provoked just now, since everything depended upon the localization of the Austro-Serbian conflict. From this Fischer inferred that "the break-up of the Entente, the chief objective of pre-war diplomacy, Bethmann Hollweg now thought to force through at any price — with or without war." Can one argue any more one-sidedly?

It is peevish to cavil over such details; but it is unavoidable, for in their accumulation they distort the picture of the reality unrecognizably for the not-well-enough-informed reader — and always unfavorably for Germany. Fischer's book reports something about two dispatches of Lichnowsky's from London on July 27, from which Grey's deep-seated ill-feeling over the German attitude became perceptible for the first time. . . . Now today it will surely occur to no one to find the attitude of Bethmann and Jagow toward the English warning politically wise and right. That up to July 29 they did not take it seriously enough and held firmly too long to the idea that they should not fail their ally and spoil for it the (apparently last) chance to establish its prestige again through a speedy military success, was a miscalculation that bordered on delusion. Why must the critic, however, be overcome by this mistake. . . ? Above all, why does Fischer try to exonerate the crafty policy of a Berchtold, as vacillating as it was flippant, to the disadvantage of Bethmann? I myself must repeat that I want to refute again the assertion (stemming from Albertini) that officials in Vienna after July 14 had "let it be known that they did not want it to come to extremes" and that only because of the forceful pressure from Berlin was Vienna led to its precipitate declaration of war, which was to end all attempts of the great powers at mediation. . . .

[Fischer] once for all firmly holds that Bethmann definitely did not want peace because he believed that he was obliged not to shun war, and he had now decided upon "a great diplomatic success" for Germany. The protestations of his love for peace were pure hypocrisy and likewise the warnings to Vienna were intended exclusively to push the responsibility for the war onto the Russians, whose need for prestige Fischer evidently finds to be as justified as that of the Central Powers was unjustified. . . .

Up to the night of July 29/30, [Bethmann] had sought to deceive England . . . and to influence her toward neutrality — although as early as the 27th Grey had "seen through the German game." And yet in the conversation with British Ambassador Goschen, in the late evening of the 29th, Bethmann had appeared as "almost sure of victory, yes, high handed"; he had even now "revealed his goal" to the Englishman: "the first steps of German war aims, which soon after the outbreak of war appeared clearly," were the overthrow of France and Belgium, the acquisition of French colonies as a continuation of the Morocco policy of 1911, and so forth. What inconceivable folly, the reader will be compelled to say, when he learns that Bethmann Hollweg had sought to win England's consent to such plans. All the more dramatic was the effect of the sudden breakdown of all hopes of British neutrality that same night when Lichnowsky's report arrived that Grey had told him England could not remain neutral in case of a Franco-German war. But tough as ever, the chancellor held firmly to his fictions. No longer for the sake of England but for that of German Social Democracy he now rushes his last pressing admonitions and warnings to Vienna. . . . Proof of the domestic political motive (the Social Democrats) was Bethmann's remark in a meeting of the Prussian cabinet on July 30 that he believed he could rely on the loyalty of the Social Democrats in case war broke out. . . .

Does not Fischer know the true reason, namely that significant conference of the chancellor with Moltke and Falkenhayn on the late evening of July 30, the tragic turning point of the whole July crisis, in which the generals convinced the resisting chancellor that it was already too late for mediation attempts and negotiations with the Russians, since according to the information of the general staff Russian total mobilization was already obviously in progress. . . ? Nevertheless Fischer appears not to believe the genuineness of these reasons. Rather, he maintains offhandedly that an excited marginal note of the Emperor on a dispatch from Petersburg, which revealed Russian partial mobilization against Austria, had removed all the previous inhibitions . . . as if eagerness for war and not burning anxiety concerning the well-timed execution of the now rigidly fixed

Schlieffen plan had prevailed at the general staff! Whoever reads the sources soberly and without bias can only shake his head at such a contrived interpretation. . . . Fischer has taken no notice of my pains to clear up the military-technical relationships. Instead, he piles up fictitious arguments in order to read into the German policy of July motives of imperialistic power and conquest. . . .

Moltke's attitude immediately before the outbreak of the war is generally pictured in a way for which the expression "biased" seems to me altogether too mild. One knows that he fell into despair when the Emperor on the evening of August 1 suddenly ordered him to stop the war in the west, which had already begun, because a remarkable telegram (quickly recognized as an error) of Lichnowsky's for a moment rekindled the hope that England would guarantee French neutrality if we renounced the idea of attacking in the west. Moltke's excitement over this unexpected disruption of his plan and over the presumptuous demand of the Emperor to turn the whole deployment toward the east, I myself have characterized as a personality failing (similar to that of Falkenhayn and Tirpitz). . . . Had Moltke followed the Emperor's command, it would only have led to awful chaos; besides Moltke got a most ungracious reception of his remonstrance by William II and the latter's just as careless as dilettantist interference in strategic decisions seemed to be evidence of distrust that deeply shocked him. No one who can read the sources impartially will understand his exclamation at this moment, "Now, it only remains for Russia to back out, too!" . . . as anything other than bitter irony. Fischer, who asserts that the Chief of the General Staff was "beside himself over the possibility of a neutral France," suggests to the reader that he was just as frightened over a "backing out of Russia" — therefore frightened (what should one infer otherwise than that?) over the maintenance of peace.

After all that, it is hardly rewarding to argue with Fischer's concluding considerations concerning "who was guilty," in which he seeks to support his thesis by the later retrospective of Tisza, Czernin, Admiral von Müller, Ballin, and Bethmann Hollweg, which he interprets as either a kind of confession of guilt, or as accusations by well-informed participants. He does not speak exactly of Germany's sole guilt, but says, cautiously and informally, that "the governments of the participating European powers in one way or another and in very different degrees shared in the responsibility for the outbreak of the World War." Since in his exposition, however, there is not a syllable about the coresponsibility of the non-German powers, it seems to me as good as excluded that any reader will interpret this background of the war as something other than a renewal of the guilt clause of Versailles. . . .

In summary, let it be said that this work for the first time has applied the thesis of Ludwig Dehio (which is as glittering as it is dangerous and is in the last analysis only a half-truth) concerning the "war for hegemony" as the essence of both world wars, in a great exposition from the sources. At the same time in Fischer a first peak is reached in today's fashionable stream of political history — the obscuring of Self in German historical consciousness that, since the catastrophe of 1945, has superseded the earlier apotheosis of Self, and now appears successfully and one-sidedly to assert itself. I am convinced that it will work out no less fatefully than the superpatriotism of former times. Thus I lay the book down not without genuine sadness — sadness and anxiety respecting the coming generation.

Paul W. Schroeder

World War I As Galloping Gertie

Paul W. Schroeder, professor of history at the University of Illinois, has published on Metternich's diplomacy, Austria and the Crimean War, and global diplomacy in 1941. In this highly revisionist article he argues that Britain in particular sought to "encircle" not Germany but Austria-Hungary, and that in 1914 the Entente powers in general were willing to cast aside the weakest link in the European system: the Danubian monarchy. In the process, they destroyed the European order. Above all, Schroeder makes a case for a less Germanocentric view of the origins of the war of 1914.

From Paul W. Schroeder, "World War I As Galloping Gertie: A Reply to Joachim Remak," *Journal of Modern History*, v. 44 (1972), pp. 319–345. Reprinted with permission of The University of Chicago Press.

To start with Fischer: most of what he says about Germany and her bid for world power is true. Many of his formulations and emphases are open to challenge. He is too hard on Bethmann-Hollweg and misinterprets the motives of his crucial decision in 1914. He often underestimates the importance and persistence of concerns other than *Weltpolitik* in German policy, and he tends to blur the difference between Germany's prewar and wartime goals in emphasizing their continuity. But these points do not destroy his main argument. From 1890 on, Germany did pursue world power. This bid arose from deep roots within Germany's economic, political, and social structures. Once the war broke out, world power became Germany's essential goal. Fischer and his students have made the old apologias for German policy impossible.

The difficulty arises in accepting the notion, implicit in all of Fischer's work and explicitly drawn by many historians as the chief lesson of it, that Germany's bid for world power was the *causa causans*, the central driving force behind the war. Fischer never demonstrates this convincingly. His case is far more informative, compelling, and reliable on Germany's policy and national character than on the origins of the war. He may be able to tell us what Germany was like without worrying much about the policies of other powers (although even here the comparative dimension is lacking). But he cannot assume, as he constantly does, that German policy was decisive for other powers without a great deal more investigation than he has done. Moreover, Fischer's own principle of *der Primat der Innenpolitik* [the primacy of internal policy] should have led him to assume that other powers would, like Germany, act mainly from their own indigenous drives, rather than mainly react to what Germany did, as he depicts them doing.

More important, the whole attempt to find a *causa causans* behind the multiplicity of contributing factors is misconceived. It is like looking for *the* driving force behind the French or Russian Revolutions, or the Reformation, or the American Civil War. Immediately, one encounters a plethora of "causes" far more than sufficient to account for the phenomenon one wishes to explain, clearly connected with it, and yet not "sufficient" in the sense that any set of them logically implies what occurred. . . . When on top of earlier valid arguments Fischer and his disciples insist that Germany's bid for world power was really behind it all, when Marxist historians insist that the war was the inevitable outcome of monopolistic capitalist imperialism, when Arno Mayer proposes domestic political and social unrest and the dynamics of counterrevolution as decisive, and when Peter Loewenberg argues in reply that this role belongs to the fundamental drives revealed by psychodynamic theory, one begins to suspect that all these approaches, however much valuable information and insight they may provide, cannot deliver what they promise. Not only is an attempt to reduce or subordinate the various contributing factors to some fundamental cause methodologically very dubious, but also, even if it worked . . . this would still not give the *causa causans.* For in the breakdown of a system of relations such as occurred in 1914 as a result of various intertwined and interacting forces, the system itself enters into the work of destruction. In the process wittily described by Hexter as "galloping Gertie,"[1] the very devices built into a system to keep it stable and operative under stress, subjected to intolerable pressures, generate forces of their own which cause the system to destroy itself.

World War I seems to me clearly a case of "Galloping Gertie." Witness how statesmen and military leaders everywhere in 1914, especially in the Central Powers, felt themselves to be in the grip of uncontrollable forces. They sensed that their calculations were all futile and that what their actions would finally produce lay beyond all calculation. . . . True, it required certain contingent events to start a war in 1914; but this does not mean the whole development was purely contingent, with nothing inevitable about it. Europe's frequent escapes from crises before 1914 do not indicate the possibility that she could have continued to avoid war indefinitely; they rather indicate a general systemic crisis, an approaching breakdown. . . .

Thus the search for the fundamental cause of World War I is futile, while the argument that the war simply happened is unhelpful. Is there no exit from the cul-de-sac? A different question may help: not Why World War I? but Why not? War was still the *ultima ratio regnum.* World War I was a normal development in international relations; events had been building toward it for a long time.

---

[1] J. H. Hexter, *The History Primer* (New York, 1970), pp. 118–135. "Galloping Gertie" was the popular name for the Tacoma Narrows Bridge in Washington, which collapsed in 1940 when winds induced pressures on supporting members sufficient in turn to cause the supports to generate destructive forces within the bridge.

There is no need to explain it as a deviation from the norm. In this sense, the question Why not? answers the question Why?

More important, it points to what is unexpected about the war and needs explanation: its long postponement. Why not until 1914? This question clearly needs answering in regard to Austria. Historians continue to exercise themselves over why the Austrian Monarchy risked its own destruction by insisting on punishing Serbia. The favorite (and very unsatisfactory) answer is that this was the kind of futile, absurd action to be expected from so decrepit an empire with so inept a ruling class. In fact, the problem is nonexistent. Preventive wars, even risky preventive wars, are not extreme anomalies in politics, the sign of the bankruptcy of policy. They are a normal, even common, tool of statecraft, right down to our own day. . . . As for the particular decision of June 1914, the evidence is plain that Berchtold, although often wavering, resisted the idea of a punitive war on Serbia until the assassination. With the death of Francis Ferdinand, leader of the peace party, Berchtold simultaneously ran out of alternatives, arguments, and support for any other policy, and gave in. The real problem is to explain why Austria waited so long and tried so many other futile devices to stop the steady deterioration of her Balkan and great-power position before resorting to force. The idea of eliminating Serbia as a political factor by conquest, occupation, or preventive war was at least sixty years old, and constantly advanced. For over two centuries Austria had lived under the brooding threat of Russian encirclement in the south. Why did she act only in the desperate situation of 1914, with all alternatives exhausted?

A similar question arises with Germany. Why, with her powerful impulse toward *Weltpolitik*, did she fail to resort to war under favorable circumstances in 1905, or 1908–09, or even 1911, and try it only in 1914, when military and political leaders alike recognized the gambling nature of the enterprise? The same question, What held her back? applies to Europe in general. . . . This essay therefore deals with the question, Why not until 1914? . . .

The most important change in European politics after 1890 . . . was that Germany lost control of the system. Who gained the initiative she lost? For a short time, Britain seemed to; but the long-range gainers were France and Russia. Their alliance, giving them greater security in Europe, freed them to pursue world policy. . . . The challenge to Britain's world leadership, coinciding with Germany's loss of control of the European system, helped conceal the latter phenomenon from the Germans themselves and contributed to their persistent belief that they could play the game of two irons in the fire and that eventually Britain would have to seek German help. . . . Far from threatening the British Empire in the 1890s, Germany hovered about Britain like an opportunistic moneylender, ready to offer her services at exorbitant rates and hoping for a favorable chance to buy into the firm. France and Russia competed directly with Britain and tried to drive her out of key positions. . . . Added to this was the rise of the United States to world power and the danger of native unrest and risings in Egypt, South Africa, Ireland, and above all India. The challenges could doubtless be met, but not by the old policy. . . .

It was therefore inevitable that Britain would meet her new problems mainly by trying to devolve some of her imperial burdens on others . . . and by trying to come to terms with her opponents. Bowing out gracefully in favor of the United States in the Western Hemisphere was easy and relatively painless; equally natural was the limited alliance with Japan. But the main answer to Britain's difficulties would have to be a deal with her chief opponents, France and Russia. . . . What held it up was not British reluctance to break with splendid isolation . . . it was the refusal of France and Russia to make a deal on terms acceptable to Britain, counting as they did on British vulnerability to make her ultimately come to them.

This suggests that there is no need to bring in the German menace to explain Britain's rapprochement with France and Russia. The Triple Entente was a natural development explicable purely in terms of the needs and aims of the three powers — especially Britain. . . . Britain's colonial agreements were not directed against Germany, but only became so because of Germany's conduct. . . . Britain did not want to encircle Germany but to protect her empire. . . . It becomes even more disingenuous to claim that Britain's ententes were not intended to apply to Europe or to hurt Germany. . . . Furthermore, even if Germany's encirclement was not a British aim, the "circling out" of Germany, her exclusion from world politics and empire, *was* Britain's goal in good measure. . . . The *Auskreisung*, which Fischer portrays as the result of German aggressiveness and blunders, was precisely the outcome British diplomacy was bent on achieving.

As to Germany's naval challenge, all the facts, old and new, can be freely acknowledged. There was a great German naval program aimed directly at Britain and designed to promote *Weltpolitik*. It undoubtedly became Britain's greatest danger (after the Franco-Russian danger faded away) and the foremost element in Anglo-German rivalry. No improvement could come in Anglo-German relations without some naval settlement. But it is one thing to see the naval challenge as a real, serious issue, sufficient to itself to compel Britain to be on guard against Germany. It is quite another to argue that it primarily shaped British policy toward Germany, or that an end to the naval race would have significantly changed British policy. . . . Of course the British were angered by Germany's naval challenge; it was expensive, gratuitous, and worrisome. But they never doubted they could meet it; it had its domestic and foreign policy uses; it was much easier to get money voted for ships than for men and supplies. . . . Above all, no naval agreement would have ended Anglo-German rivalry or caused Britain to abandon the anti-German coalition. . . .

Of course Germany played world policy. . . . The point is how Germany played it. Somehow Fischer never quite succeeds in explaining the contrast between the remarkable growth of Germany's power and wealth and her uniform failure to translate that power into corresponding diplomatic, political, and territorial gains. . . . The main reason for Germany's failure is not ineptness and aggressiveness, or her late start in Weltpolitik, or even unfavorable geography, although these are involved. It is that Germany could not pursue Weltpolitik all out. Each of the Entente powers could carry on a world policy without directly overthrowing the European system . . . but an unrestrained Weltpolitik by Germany, as the Germans were forced to recognize, was bound to isolate her and destroy the system upon which she had to rely for security as much as upon her army. Thus the exigencies of continental policy repeatedly imposed themselves upon Germany and restrained her.

This explains what most needs explaining about prewar German policy. The problem is not, as is often imagined, one of accounting for her reckless conduct in terms of her aggressive, imperialist character and aims. It is one of accounting for the surprising moderation of German policy until 1914, in view of her aggressive character and aims. . . . The contradiction between what Germany wanted to do and what she dared do and was obliged to do accounts in turn for the erratic, uncoordinated character of German world policy, its inability to settle on clear goals and carry them through, the constant initiatives leading nowhere, the frequent changes in mid-course. It is commonly said that after 1890 Germany played the game of international politics like a plunger on the stock market, always looking for quick short-term gains. The truth is worse than this. Germany played it like a plunger looking for quick gains without making any investments, a gambler trying to win without betting. The Germans were always hoping to be paid for doing nothing, merely for being where they were; expecting to be feared and to have their interests respected because of the power they possessed but dared not exert. . . . Disappointed, the Germans wondered with querulous self-pity why everyone was against them — the same mood they had often expressed before unification, and which would become the national disease after 1918. . . .

Britain wanted to keep Germany from dominating the continent by either overpowering France and Russia or luring them into her camp. This was entirely legitimate and necessary, but it alone is not enough to make Britain's a real balance-of-power policy. For . . . the important point is that the British neither recognized nor did anything about the most critical threat to the European balance after 1900, but helped make it much worse. . . . The greatest danger stemmed not from German or Russian power but from Austrian weakness. One of the few incontestable points in balance-of-power theory is that preserving the system means preserving all the essential actors in it. Equally obvious, nothing is more likely to occasion a major war than a threat to the existence or great-power status of an essential actor. . . . Long before 1914 it was obvious that Austria's existence was threatened. Everyone saw her as the next sick man of Europe after Turkey. . . . From 1908 on almost everyone anticipated the long-awaited general war would probably arise over a Russo-Austrian quarrel involving Serbia. From 1912 on the Russians and Serbs repeatedly told their Western friends that Austria's collapse was imminent, and that they intended to have the lion's share of the remains.

Yet Britain's "balance-of-power" policy entirely ignored this immediate danger, and served actually to increase the threat from Germany as well. Germany . . . was virtually bound to accept war, even provoke it, rather than let Austria go under and thus lose her last reliable ally. . . . A real balance-of-power policy would have required from the Entente . . . a policy of restraint for themselves and controlled support for Austria. . . . The threat to Austria . . . was a product in great part of Entente policy. As a result of the preoccupation of diplomatic historians with motives and aims instead of effects, both German and Entente policies have always been discussed almost exclusively in terms of the German problem, when in fact their effects were far greater on the Austrian problem. The best answer to the German encirclement myth is not that Entente policy was really moderate and unprovocative; there has been too much white-washing of British, French, and especially Russian policy in this whole debate. The answer is rather that the Entente really encircled Austria rather than Germany. . . . Austria . . . was hopelessly encircled by 1914 and knew it. Russia, supported by France, was forming a new Balkan League around Russia's protégé and Austria's worst enemy, Serbia. Rumania was defecting, Bulgaria was exhausted and wavering under strong Russo-French pressure, Turkey was leaning toward Russia, Italy was cooperating with Russia in the Balkans; even Germany was a wholly unreliable support politically, and Austria's chief competitor economically in the Balkans.

This isolation and encirclement resulted, moreover, principally from Entente moves and policies, always discussed as if they had nothing to do with Austria. . . . Austria was . . . the actual target of Entente diplomacy. . . . In fact, one can argue that Britain's policy (like Russia's and even, in certain respects, France's) was more anti-Austrian than anti-German. . . . [The British] never took Austria seriously and were regularly ready to let her pay, or make her pay. . . . [Britain] urged Russia to concentrate her power and attention on Europe, telling her that with time and patience she could become the arbiter of Europe — the worst possible threat to Austria. The British . . . worked to break up the long-standing Austro-Russian cooperation in Macedonia, valuable though they knew it to be for European peace. . . . When Austria annexed Bosnia, legalizing a situation long existing de facto and giving up her hold on the Sanjak of Novi-Bazar in the process, Britain helped promote an international crisis over the violation of a treaty thirty years old, whose relevant provision had never been intended by Britain herself to remain long in force. . . .

On the eve of the war, the Foreign Office was aware of the fear prevalent in both Berlin and Vienna that Austria might collapse. Far from viewing this eventuality as a danger per se . . . Grey feared rather what actually happened: a preventive war launched by Germany out of fear of Russia's growing strength and Austria's decline. . . . No thought of any action to help maintain Austria's independence and integrity was entertained. . . . Of course there was no great anti-Austrian plot. The British did not think of Austria as their enemy; they tried not to think of her at all. They did not plan to isolate and destroy her; they simply did not concern themselves . . . with the question of whether the concessions and defeats forced upon Austria before the war, and the territorial sacrifices to be imposed on her during and after it, would leave her viable. Britain undermined Austria's position before the war . . . and assisted in her destruction during it, in a fit of absence of mind, a state from which many British historians on this subject have not yet emerged. . . . What makes Britain's responsibility for Austria's plight a heavy one, although less direct than Russia's or France's, is that Britain alone was in a position to manage the European Concert so as to control the Balkan situation. . . . Only the presence of the Habsburg Monarchy holding down the Danube basin kept Germany or Russia from achieving mastery over Europe. . . . Let Austria go under, and a great war for the mastery of Europe became almost mathematically predictable. . . .

The basic point is that everyone saw the central threat to the European system in the decline of Austria, and no one would do anything about it. Russians, Serbs, Rumanians, Greeks, and Italians all exploited it; the French thought only of their security. Even Germany made the problem worse, by promoting Austria's survival not as a European independent great power, but as a German state and Germany's satellite. . . . The British, meanwhile, did not want Austria to die, but hoped that if she must, she would at least do it quietly. In 1914 Austria decided not to die quietly, and once this long-postponed decision to recover her position by violence was taken, there was no stopping short of a general holocaust. . . .

The attitudes behind it all, in any case, were universal — the same short-sighted selfishness and lack of imagination, the same exclusive concentration on one's own interests at the expense of the community. Everyone wanted a payoff; no one wanted to pay. Everyone expected the system to work for him; no one would work for it. All were playing the same game — imperialism, world policy, *Realpolitik*, call it what you will — all save Austria, and she also would have played it had she been able. . . . And so the system was bent and twisted until it broke. . . . Inevitably the collapse came where all the weight was concentrated — at the weakest point. Two titles from Nietzsche and Nestroy sum the whole process up: "Menschlich, allzu menschlich," and "Gegen Torheit gibt es kein Mittel." ["Human, all too human," and "There is no remedy for stupidity."]

The Legacy: Conveyor-belt death. (The Granger Collection)

IV The Legacy

Holger H. Herwig

Patriotic Self-Censorship in Germany

Holger H. Herwig, professor of history at the University of Calgary, is the author of, among other books, *Politics of Frustration: The United States in German Strategic Planning, 1889–1941*; *"Luxury" Fleet: The Imperial German Navy, 1888–1918*; and *Hammer or Anvil? Modern Germany, 1648–Present*. In this selection, he investigates how both government officials and private citizens distorted the record on Germany's role in the July crisis of 1914, and how they conducted personal

From Holger H. Herwig, "Clio Deceived: Patriotic Self-Censorship in Germany After the Great War," *International Security*, vol. 12 (Fall 1987), pp. 5–44. Reprinted by permission of MIT Press and President and Fellows of Harvard College and the Massachusetts Institute of Technology.

vendettas against radical scholars. Herwig draws conclusions concerning the effectiveness of such self-censorship.

Joseph Fouché, a man for all seasons who served the Directory, Consulate, Empire, and Restoration as minister of police, was once reputed to have stated that any two lines from any *oeuvre* would suffice to have its author hanged. Indeed, the efforts of various Germans, both in official and private capacities, to undertake what John Röhl has termed "patriotic self-censorship" with regard to the origins of the Great War reflect the sentiment expressed by the great French censor a century earlier. For nearly fifty years, until Fritz Fischer's *Griff nach der Weltmacht* appeared in 1961, which in many ways offered German readers the findings of the Italian author Luigi Albertini, the German interpretation of the origins of the First World War was dominated in large measure by the efforts of "patriotic self-censors." . . .

This article will trace the genesis and course of the official campaign in the Weimar Republic (and beyond) to counter Allied charges of German war guilt (Article 231 of the Treaty of Versailles), and offer some suggestions concerning its impact upon subsequent German affairs. The inquiry will show that the German government as early as 1914, and especially during the period from November 1918 to June 1919, sought to "organize" materials in order to answer questions concerning the origins of the war. Further, it will show that from June 1919 through the Third Reich, key elements of the German bureaucracy mounted a massive and successful campaign of disinformation that purveyed false propaganda through a wide range of channels. These included the War Guilt Section . . . of the Foreign Ministry, which disseminated its official stance on war guilt most notably through two agencies which it recruited to this end — the Working Committee of German Associations . . . and the Center for the Study of the Causes of the War . . . — as well as a parliamentary Committee of Enquiry. . . . Writers were also engaged either directly or indirectly by the Foreign Ministry to propagate its views, to organize translations of foreign studies sympathetic to the German cause, and to channel the Wilhelmstrasse's official line to German schools and diplomatic missions via newspapers and radio. . . .

By selectively editing documentary collections, suppressing honest scholarship, subsidizing pseudo-scholarship, underwriting mass propaganda, and overseeing the export of this propaganda especially to Britain, France, and the United States, the patriotic self-censors in Berlin exerted a powerful influence on public and elite opinion in Germany and, to a lesser extent, outside Germany. Their efforts polluted historical understanding both at home and abroad well into the post-1945 period. . . .

The significance of the campaign of official and semi-official obfuscation and perversion of fact extends well beyond the history of Germany or the origins of the Great War. It raises basic questions concerning the role of the historian in society, scholarly integrity, decency, and public morality. It further illustrates the universal problem of establishing the critical record of events that are sufficiently vital to the national interest to become the objects of partisan propaganda. What is the present generation, for example, to make of the collective and concerted efforts of eminent German scholars purposefully to distort their countrymen's study of history and sociology of knowledge? Does a perverse law operate whereby those events that are most important are hardest to understand because they attract the greatest attention from mythmakers and charlatans? And is a nation well-served when its intellectual establishment conspires to obstruct honest investigation into national catastrophies, upon which past, present, and future vital national interests can be reassessed? The far-reaching effects of the resulting disinformation are incalculable.

Several other related issues require to be addressed tangentially. Nazi expansionism clearly fed upon the fertile intellectual basis laid down for it by the patriotic self-censors in the 1920s. In other words, Adolf Hitler's radical "revisionism" was already well-rooted in public and elite opinion under the Weimar Republic. Finally, the export of this propaganda to Britain, France, and the United States did its part, however major or minor, to undermine the moral and eventually the strategic terms of the settlement of 1919.

Last but not least, my investigation bears directly upon the nature and meaning of the "1914 analogy," which continues to influence political science thought on the possible causes of a third world war. I suggest that the history upon which that analogy was based has been distorted. It serves no purpose to continue to believe that

Europe "slid" into war unknowingly in 1914, that no nation harbored aggressive tendencies during the July crisis, and that fate or providence alone designed this cruel course of events. Indeed, the "1914 analogy" ought to be rethought and reworked in light of the actual mindset of German political, diplomatic, and military leaders in 1914. . . .

[The] campaign [of patriotic self-censorship] was directed by what one historian has called the "general staff of the war-guilt struggle. " . . . Chief of this "general staff" was . . . [Bernhard W. von] Bülow. . . . Bülow, who had gone off to assist [Foreign Minister] Brockdorff-Rantzau at Paris, was of course fully aware of the delicate nature of his task. As he returned official diplomatic records to Berlin, he instructed . . . Hans Freytag to lock them up in a special safe so that "in case the entente should demand them" . . . "they can be got out of the way easily." And in assembling his documents, Bülow . . . informed Freytag that "any nation can be charged successfully on the basis of its documents." . . . In keeping with this spirit of selection, Bülow divided the documents that he assembled into two categories, marked "defense" and "offense. " . . .

The Wilhelmstrasse . . . devised a long-term project to publish its records from before 1914 in order to buttress its rejection of Article 231. . . . Such a broad investigation offered the additional prospect of shifting attention from the immediate causes of the Great War to a less sensitive debate about European affairs in general over the past four decades. . . .

The end result was simply staggering in terms of labor and productivity: in just over six years, the three editors brought out forty volumes (in 54 parts) of documents pertaining to European affairs before 1914. Published between 1922 and 1927, *Die Grosse Politik der Europäischen Kabinette, 1871–1914,* . . . "established an early dependence of all students of prewar diplomacy on German materials." . . .

The most obvious shortcoming of *Die Grosse Politik* stemmed from its very nature as a publication from the files of the former Foreign Office. In other words, the collection does not include the highly important, indeed critical, materials of several other, powerful planning agencies: the General Staff, the War Ministry, the Navy Office, and the bureaus responsible for economic preparations for the war. This is especially unfortunate in the case of the General Staff and the War Ministry as their files were almost totally destroyed by that greatest of "censors," the Anglo-American Bomber Command. . . . Above all, the Kaiser's incriminating marginal comments on official documents, which [Karl] Kautsky gleefully stated showed the monarch in his "underwear," remained largely unpublished. . . . Imanuel Geiss has shown that with specific reference to the July 1914 crisis that the editors failed to include (perhaps destroyed) a number of utterly critical documents. . . . [The editors] managed to defuse some potentially incriminating statements by Chancellor Theobald von Bethmann Hollweg simply by decreeing that the materials in question be returned to the family as "private" correspondence. . . .

Perhaps of interest . . . is the care lavished upon certain American scholars by the Foreign Ministry and its agents. . . . The Foreign Ministry purchased 250 copies of [Sidney B.] Fay's sympathetic two-volume *The Origins of the War* and had its diplomatic representatives overseas distribute the books free of charge. . . . In time, the Foreign Ministry funded both a German and a French translation of Fay's study. By contrast, Bernadotte Schmitt's critical *The Coming of the War 1914* was never translated into German. . . . The greatest attention and support was showered upon Harry E. Barnes. . . . [The Center for the Study of the Causes of the War] provided Barnes with research materials, propagated his writings, and funded his visits to Berlin, Munich, and Vienna in 1926. The German embassy at Washington presented him with all forty volumes of *Die Grosse Politik*. . . . Barnes's *Genesis* [of the World War was] translated into German [and] French. . . .

[A] special parliamentary Committee of Enquiry . . . invited . . . Field Marshal von Hindenburg to "testify" on November 18, 1919. It was a triumphant farce. The army provided an honor guard at the train station, two officers served as adjutants, and a guard detail was stationed at Villa Helfferich where the field marshal resided while in the capital. When Hindenburg, in full dress uniform, arrived to testify on November 18, the chamber was packed. All rose to their feet as he strode in to take his chrysanthemum-bedecked chair. There were no questions, no cross-examination. Instead, the field marshal read a brief prepared statement wherein he blamed the military defeat . . . "stabbed in the back" . . . [on] certain pacifist and socialist elements at the home front. Therewith, a legend was officially born. . . .

The case of Hermann Kantorowicz in many ways symbolizes the entire campaign of "preemptive historiography." Charged with investigating the legal parameters of the war's origins . . . Kantorowicz attributed responsibility for the war primarily to the Central Powers: Austria-Hungary for the aggressive manner in which it had launched the Balkan war with Serbia, and Germany not only for supporting the Habsburg initiative but also for rejecting all peace efforts undertaken by England and Russia after the assassination at Sarajevo. Jew, Anglophile, pacifist, republican, and democrat, Kantorowicz was accused of "fouling his own nest" [and the] . . . Prussian Cultural Minister Carl Becker informed the German Foreign Ministry of widespread opposition to Kantorowicz's recent selection to a chair [at] Kiel University. . . . The Wilhelmstrasse denied Kantorowicz private publication of his findings . . . [and] the Finance Ministry at this point rejoined the revisionist campaign by refusing to make available . . . the agreed-upon printing subsidy of 40–50,000 Mark. . . . In 1933, his name was on the list of the first 25 professors to be dismissed from university posts by the Hitler regime. . . .

To be sure, the vendetta conducted against Kantorowicz would not remain an isolated case. In 1932, several German historians . . . conspired to deny the young radical scholar Eckart Kehr the Rockefeller Fellowship that Charles A. Beard had helped Kehr secure for study in the United States. And as recently as February 1964, West Germany's Foreign Minister, Gerhard Schröder, acting upon the recommendations of Gerhard Ritter and Karl Dietrich Erdmann, formally rescinded Goethe Institute travel funds awarded Fritz Fischer for a planned lecture tour of the United States, a tour that Ritter equated with "a national tragedy." . . .

I will conclude this overview of how Clio was deceived in Germany by suggesting that the moral and institutional lessons to be learned have not lost any of their crispness and validity over the decades. Miscalculated risks are rarely glossed over simply by selectively editing pertinent documents. . . . "Preemptive historiography" may succeed in the short run; over time, it is likely to be uncovered as the sham that it is. In the final analysis, it was nothing short of a tragedy that, in the words of Hermann Hesse, "90 or 100 prominent men" conspired in the supposed interests of the state "to deceive the people on this vital question of national interest." Nor was Hesse in doubt as to the effectiveness of the campaign of "patriotic self-censorship," informing Thomas Mann in 1931 of his opinion that "of 1,000 Germans, even today 999 still know nothing of [our] war guilt." Little wonder, then, that Fritz Fischer's *Griff nach der Weltmacht* had such an explosive impact precisely thirty years later.

Suggestions for Additional Reading

The literature on the background of the First World War in general and on the July crisis of 1914 in particular is truly staggering. Vladimir Dedijer claims that more than 3,000 books exist on the events at Sarajevo on 28 June 1914 and their immediate aftermath alone. Moreover, countless anthologies offer suggestions for readings. Among these, the student may wish to consult Dwight E. Lee's "Suggestions for Additional Reading" in the fourth edition of this book, *The Outbreak of the First World War: Causes and Responsibilities* (Lexington, Mass., 1975). The older works of Albertini, Barnes, Fay, Schmitt, and Wegerer, among others, are listed there; it would be redundant to cite these again.

Of the numerous anthologies published recently on the origins of the Great War, the latest entry in the field comes from two British scholars: R. J. W. Evans and Hartmut Pogge von Strandmann, eds., *The Coming of the First World War* (Oxford, 1988). After an introductory survey "Europe on the Eve of the First World War," by Michael Howard (excerpted in this book), the collection offers essays on the Balkans (Z. A. B. Zeman), the Habsburgs in Austria (R. J. W. Evans), Russia (D. W. Spring), Germany (Hartmut Pogge von Strandmann), France (Richard Cobb), and Britain (Michael Block).

Several general surveys of Europe prior to 1914 have stood the test of time: William L. Langer, *European Alliances and Alignments, 1870–1890* (New York, 1933), and *The Diplomacy of Imperialism* (2 vols.; New York, 1951); Pierre Renouvin, *L'Epoque contemporaine*, vol. 2, *La Paix Armée et la Grand Guerre, 1871–1919* (Paris, 1953), and *La Crise européenne et la Première Guerre Mondiale* (Paris, 1962); as well as A. J. P. Taylor, *The Struggle for Mastery in Europe 1848–1918* (Oxford, 1954). Dwight E. Lee, *Europe's Crucial Years: The Diplomatic Background of World War I, 1902–1914* (Hanover, N.H., 1974), includes a bibliography that updates those of the works cited above.

With regard to the "mood of 1914," the reader would do well to consult James Joll's superb collection, *The Origins of the First World War* (London and New York, 1984), which contains not only the article ("The Mood of 1914") excerpted in this book, but also prescient pieces on the alliance system, imperial rivalries, militarism, and the primacy of domestic politics.

The rich monographic literature published in the past two decades dealing with the foreign and domestic policies of the great powers of Europe has been conveniently synthesized in a number of inexpensive paperbacks in the series *The Making of the 20th Century*, edited by St. Martin's Press, New York, including: V. R. Berghahn, *Germany and the Approach of War in 1914* (1973); Zara S. Steiner, *Britain and the Origins of the First World War* (1977) (excerpted in this volume); Richard J. B. Bosworth, *Italy and the Approach of the First World War* (1983); John F. V. Keiger, *France and the Origins of the First World War* (1983); D. C. B. Lieven, *Russia and the Origins of the First World War* (1983) (excerpted in this volume), and Samuel R. Williamson, Jr., *Austria-Hungary and the Origins of the First World War* (1991).

The publication of Fritz Fischer's *Griff nach der Weltmacht. Die Kriegszielpolitik des kaiserlichen Deutschland 1914/18* in 1961 was a watershed in the debate concerning the history of the origins of the Great War. This highly provocative work delineated the parameters of the debate, ushered in a period of feverish archival research, and brought forth a flood of fresh evaluations. Volker R. Berghahn has suggested that the dispute over the origins of *La Grand Guerre* has been clarified in at least one central point as a result of Fischer's labors: one no longer needs to go on an extended tour of Europe's capitals in search of those responsible; scholars today can concentrate on the documents from the files that piled up in Berlin and Vienna. With the exception of L. C. F. Turner *Origins of the First World War* (New York, 1967), who has focused on Russia as the main culprit, contemporary scholars are in general agreement that the July crisis originated in and was orchestrated by, at least in its initial stages, Austria-Hungary and Germany. To a considerable degree, the passion of the debate and the acrimony of the controversy have now abated sufficiently to indicate at least some of the major contributions on both sides of the "Fischer controversy."

Fischer's *magnum opus* was translated into English in shortened form as *Germany's Aims in the First World War* (New York, 1967). The storm of protest that it aroused prompted the Hamburg historian to postulate his views in even sharper contours in *Krieg der Illusionen. Die deutsche Politik von 1911 bis 1914* (Düsseldorf, 1969), which again was translated into English in abridged form as *War of Illusions: German Policies from 1911 to 1914* (New York, 1975). Without diminishing Fischer's central role in the debate one iota, it nevertheless should be pointed out that he owed a major intellectual debt to the Italian journalist Luigi Albertini and his work, *The Origins of the War of 1914* (3 vols.; New York, 1952–1957), originally published in Italian as *Le origini della guerra del 1914* (3 vols.; Milan, 1942–1943).

A good deal of the archival work in Berlin and Vienna pertaining to the July crisis of 1914 was done by Fischer's students — including the research for various chapters of *Griff nach der Weltmacht* — as well as by other historians sympathetic to his findings. First and foremost, his student Imanuel Geiss published much of the pertinent diplomatic record: *Julikrise und Kriegsausbruch 1914. Eine Dokumentensammlung* (2 vols.; Hanover, 1963–1964); a much-shortened version (about one-third of the German material) appeared as *July 1914: The Outbreak of the First World War. Selected Documents* (New York, 1968). Geiss initially offered his major conclusions to English-language readers in "The Outbreak of the First World War and German War Aims," *Journal of Contemporary History* 1 (July 1966), pp. 75–91, excerpted in this volume. Adolf Gasser has gone perhaps furthest in claiming that Germany purposefully launched a preventive war in 1914, in several articles, none of which have been translated into English: "Deutschlands Entschluss zum Präventivkrieg 1913–1914," in *Discordia Concors. Festgabe für Edgar Bonjour zu seinem siebzigsten Geburtstag am 21. August 1968* (2 vols.; Basel, 1968), pp. 171–224, reprinted in Adolf Gasser, *Ausgewählte historische Schriften* (Basel, 1983), pp. 1–46; and "Der deutsche Hegemonialkrieg von 1914," in Imanuel Geiss and Bernd Jürgen Wendt, eds., *Deutschland in der Weltpolitik des 19. und 20. Jahrhunderts. Fritz Fischer zum 65. Geburtstag* (Düsseldorf, 1973), pp. 307–339.

John C. G. Röhl of Sussex University, United Kingdom, has taken Fischer's side with *1914: Delusion or Design? The Testimony of Two German diplomats* (New York, 1973) (excerpted in this volume); and "Admiral von Müller and the Approach of War, 1911–1914," *Historical Journal* 12 (1969), pp. 651–673.

The major attacks on Fischer, not surprisingly, came from conservative historians in the Federal Republic of Germany. Egmont

Zechlin, his colleague at Hamburg University, attacked Fischer in a booklength article: "Deutschland zwischen Kabinettskrieg und Wirtschaftskrieg. Politik und Kriegführung in den ersten Monaten des Weltkrieges 1914," *Historische Zeitschrift* 199 (1964), pp. 247–458. Zechlin's numerous writings on the First World War have been collected as Egmont Zechlin, *Krieg und Kriegsrisiko. Zur deutschen Politik im 1. Weltkrieg. Aufsätze* (Düsseldorf, 1979). The late Gerhard Ritter of Freiburg University became Fischer's most persistent critic and devoted the third volume of his magisterial *Staatskunst und Kriegshandwerk. Das Problem des "Militarismus" in Deutschland* (4 vols.; Munich, 1964–1968) — in English translation, *The Sword and the Scepter: The Problem of Militarism in Germany* (4 vols.; Coral Gables, 1969–1972) — to the wartime chancellorship of Bethmann Hollweg in order to refute Fischer's interpretation. Ritter's lengthy review of Fischer's first book in the *Historische Zeitschrift* (1962) is excerpted in this volume. The late Andreas Hillgruber of Cologne University joined the fray against Fischer by reasserting the validity of the thesis that Germany undertook no more than a "calculated risk" in 1914: "Riezlers Theorie des kalkulierten Risikos und Bethmann Hollwegs politische Konzeption in der Julikrise 1914," *Historische Zeitschrift* 202 (1966), pp. 333–351. Hillgruber's position was largely echoed in the United States by Konrad H. Jarausch, "The Illusion of Limited War: Chancellor Bethmann Hollweg's Calculated Risk, July 1914," *Central European History* 2 (March 1969), pp. 48–76.

John A. Moses, *The War Aims of Imperial Germany: Professor Fritz Fischer and His Critics*, University of Queensland Papers, Department of Government and Politics, 1 (1968), offered an interim balance in the debate. The indefatigable Imanuel Geiss [ed., *Die Fischer-Kontroverse. Ein kritischer Beitrag zum Verhältnis zwischen Historiographie und Politik in der Bundesrepublik* (Frankfurt, 1972)], sought to place the "Fischer controversy" in the larger picture of the self-image of the Bonn regime in the wake of the Second World War. Most recently, Holger H. Herwig, in "Clio Deceived: Patriotic Self-Censorship in Germany After the Great War," *International Security* 12 (Fall 1987), pp. 5–44, excerpted in this book, has presented an analysis of how both official and semiofficial circles in Germany sought to combat the so-called "war-guilt lie" after 1919, and how in the process they distorted historical knowledge.

The "Fischer controversy" entered a new phase of intensity with the publication of the papers of Bethmann Hollweg's adviser in the German Foreign Office, Kurt Riezler [Karl Dietrich Erdmann, ed., *Kurt Riezler. Tagebücher, Aufsätze, Dokumente* (Göttingen, 1972)]. Riezler's papers were evaluated for the English-language reader first by Fritz Stern, "Bethmann Hollweg and the War: The Bounds of Responsibility," and "German Historians and the War: Fritz Fischer and His Critics"; both articles appeared in Fritz Stern, ed., *The Failure of Illiberalism: Essays on the Political Culture of Modern Germany* (New York, 1972), pp. 77–118, 147–158. An in-depth treatment of Riezler's career is now available from Wayne C. Thompson, *In the Eye of the Storm: Kurt Riezler and the Crises of Modern Germany* (Iowa City, 1980) (excerpted in this volume). The debate as to whether the Riezler papers were in fact edited by Erdmann in an attempt to remove possibly incriminating passages for the critical days of July 1914 is analyzed by Bernd F. Schulte, *Die Verfälschung der Riezler Tagebücher. Ein Beitrag zur Wissenschaftsgeschichte der 50er und 60er Jahre* (Frankfurt, 1985).

Civilian-military relations in general and strategic planning in particular have also received their share of scholarly attention. Samuel R. Williamson, Jr.'s *The Politics of Grand Strategy: Britain and France Prepare for War, 1904–1914* (Cambridge, Mass., 1969) has become the standard in the field. John Gooch, *The Plans of War: The General Staff and British Military Strategy, c. 1900–1916* (London, 1974), analyzes the genesis of Britain's continental commitment, while Douglas Porch, *The March to the Marne: The French Army, 1871–1914* (Cambridge, 1981), challenges many of the standard assumptions about the place of the army in the Republic's political life. William C. Fuller, Jr., *Civil-Military Conflict in Imperial Russia, 1881–1914* (Princeton, 1985), has provided the first full-scale study in English of civil-military relations in the last decades of the Imperial period, arguing that on the eve of the First World War, the interests of the army were divisible from those of the tsarist regime. John Whittam, *The Politics of the Italian Army, 1861–1918* (London, 1977), offers an overview of one of the lesser powers that eventually became involved in the war; John Gooch, *Army, State, and Society in Italy, 1870–1915* (New York, 1989), sheds more light on the nature of the Italian military.

With regard to the Dual Monarchy, Graydon A. Tunstall, *Plan-*

ning for War Against Russia and Serbia: Austro-Hungarian and German Military Strategies, 1871–1914 (New York, 1993), provides the first cogent analysis of Habsburg military planning before 1914. The massive memoir of the Austro-Hungarian Chief of the General Staff, Franz Baron Conrad von Hötzendorf, *Aus meiner Dienstzeit, 1906–1918* (5 vols., Vienna, Leipzig, and Munich, 1925), is beyond the reach of most students. Works on German military planning include Ritter's four-volume *Sword and Scepter*, cited earlier, as well as his classic *Der Schlieffenplan: Kritik eines Mythos* (Munich, 1956) — also available in English as *The Schlieffen Plan: Critique of a Myth* (Westport, Conn., 1979). L. L. Farrar, Jr., *The Short-War Illusion: German Policy, Strategy and Domestic Affairs August–December 1914* (Santa Barbara and Oxford, 1973), excerpted in this volume, provides an intriguing insight into why leaders in Berlin proved willing to accept war so readily in 1914.

Last but not least, four anthologies offer fresh interpretations of the military side of the war. Paul M. Kennedy, ed., *The War Plans of the Great Powers, 1880–1914* (London, 1979), serves up succinct pieces on Joffre and French strategy (Samuel R. Williamson), the Schlieffen plan (L. C. F. Turner), Generals Moltke and Conrad (Norman Stone), and the Russian mobilisation in 1914 (L. C. F. Turner). Emest R. May, ed., *Knowing One's Enemies: Intelligence Assessment Before the Two World Wars* (Princeton, 1984), offers evaluations of military-intelligence assessment before the First World War in Austria-Hungary (Norman Stone), Germany (Holger H. Herwig), Russia (William C. Fuller), France (Christopher M. Andrew and Jan K. Tanenbaum), Great Britain (Paul Kennedy), and Italy (John Gooch). The actual performance of European armies both before and during the Great War has been scrutinized in Allan R. Millett and Williamson Murray, eds., *Military Effectiveness*, vol. l, *The First World War* (Boston, 1988). Finally, a fresh look at diplomacy and strategy is provided by Williamson Murray, MacGregor Knox, and Alvin Bernstein, eds., *The Making of Strategy: Rulers, States, and War* (New York, 1994); Brian R. Sullivan deals with Italy, John Gooch with Britain, and Holger H. Herwig with Germany.

An interpretation of the devastating impact of *La Grand Guerre* upon Europe in the twentieth century is provided by Modris Eksteins, *Rites of Spring: The Great War and the Birth of the Modern Age* (New York, 1989).